Daniel Lane is an award-winning sports journalist. His previous
books include *Rugby League Rebel—The Mark Geyer Story*
(1994), *Laurie and Clyde, Young Guns of Rugby League* (1995),
*A Family Betrayal* with Jarrod McCracken (1996), *Sirro! Tales
From Tigertown* (1997), *Pacemaker* with Glenn McGrath (1998)
and *Raging Waters: The Life of an Innocent Killer* (1998) with
Dean Waters.

Lane spent time training with the Waters boys on their
Kulnura property when he prepared to fight as an amateur
heavyweight. However, he earned the wrath of Ces Waters
when he openly supported Guy's move to Johnny Lewis' stable
of boxers at the Newtown Police Boys Club.

Lane lives in Sydney.

# THE MAN

# THE MAN

## ANTHONY MUNDINE

### WITH DANIEL LANE

MACMILLAN
Pan Macmillan Australia

First published 2000 in Macmillan by Pan Macmillan Australia Pty Limited
St Martins Tower, 31 Market Street, Sydney

National Library of Australia
Cataloguing-in-Publication data:

Mundine, Anthony.
The man.

ISBN 0 7329 1044 7.

1. Mundine, Anthony. 2. Rugby League football players –
Australia – Biography. 3. Rugby League football –
Australia – Biography. 4. Aboriginal Australian Rugby
League football players – Biography. I. Lane, Daniel
(Daniel Q.). II. Title.

796.3338092

Typeset in 11/15 pt Garamond by Post Pre-press Group
Printed in Australia by McPherson's Printing Group

# CONTENTS

# FAMILY
# AND
# FRIENDS

# CHAPTER 1

# FAMILY TIES

I remember Grandma Audrey. She was a sweet, kindly black woman and I was the favourite of all her grandkids. She was the person who christened me 'Choc' when I was just a baby and my face was painted an even darker shade of brown by the piece of chocolate I was sucking on. She looked at me and laughed; she called me a 'l'le chocolate baby' and kissed me gently. That was my second baptism, because from then on I answered to 'Choc' and I'm real proud the name she gave me is renowned throughout Australian sport—in a small way, it helps to keep a special piece of Grandma Audrey alive in my heart.

While I have no doubt I inherited some of my father's world title class boxing skills, I like to think I have a healthy dose of Grandma's gumption. She was a strong woman who lived a tough life. Her spine was damaged when my uncle Lionel was born and she lost the use of a leg as a result. She didn't have a flash pad either. Grandma Audrey raised nine kids in a shack Poppa Mundine built and it was Spartan, to say the least. Five kids slept in one room and they didn't have any beds; all of them, my father, Tony, included, bunked down on the floor. No electricity or plumbing either. When Grandma Audrey had to wash she'd drag herself down to the creek and sit there from daylight to dusk, and then she'd drag herself home through the prickly grass and dirt. In the end her arm became badly infected and the doctors at the hospital—Grafton, I think—had to amputate it. I remember her as an extremely proud woman. And from hearing Dad and my uncles talk, I know she did her utmost to give her children a good life amid the poverty and hopelessness of the tin-shed town of Baryulgil on the far north coast of New South Wales. Grandma knew grief too, brother. She saw a daughter and most of the men in her family die long before their time. The fellas died as a result of working in the asbestos mines, where they swung fourteen-pound sledgehammers from sunup to sundown.

Poppa Mundine was a good man. I can remember going to the park with him as a little boy to play. However, he had a problem with the bottle—the grog—and it cursed him with the same demons which have plagued so many members of my race. Yet, while I have followed my dad's lead and am anti-alcohol and drugs, I don't judge Poppa Mundine, because he endured things in his life I haven't had to deal with—the deaths of his brothers and friends, in-his-face racism and the awful feeling of belonging to what is perceived to be an inferior class. He was a good man and I loved him, and I know he loved all of us.

Mum's family came from the western town of Wellington and they lived away from the township on a farm, though it was by no means an easy life. Mum's mother, my grandmother, Eileen McGuinness, was also a member of the stolen generations, and what eats at Mum and me is having seen the documentation noting her being taken away for 'reasons unknown'. It hurts. We've tried to find Grandma Eileen's family, but it's close to impossible because no paperwork seems to exist. My uncles and Mum have been searching for the missing part of our family since 1984, and it burns at each of us that we seem destined to go through our lives not knowing our extended family. It's the type of thing which has damaged the Aboriginal psyche. My mother's lines are mixed blood, and I remember whenever our whole clan was together there was a tremendous feeling of love and togetherness. It was a special bond, brother, and there are times I would give up everything just to be able to enjoy the warmth we all experienced when my grandparents, parents, sister Kelly, uncles, aunts and cousins got together.

The greatest influences on my life have been my father and my mother, Lynette. I love Mum with all my heart, as she's helped make me the person I am. However, I always wanted to walk in my dad's footsteps. He was—is—The Man. The way I saw him through my child's eyes was the way I wanted to be. I don't know why I was never called Tony. Perhaps it was done out of respect for my father; maybe it was done to let me grow into being my own man. Yet even so, I'd be proud to grow into the type of man Dad is. He has self-respect and he was always a solid citizen. He knew what it was like to be poor too, because at thirteen he left school to work as a woodchopper, a ringbarker, a cattle brander. He built fences and swung a heavy sledgehammer in the asbestos mines, taking his place alongside the other men in his clan. Dad was drawn by the bright lights of Sydney and found fame as a boxer, earning the admiration of millions of people here and overseas through his ability to win titles with powerful blows—blows which could jolt an opponent as if they'd been zapped by 140 volts of electricity!

However, in this country, which scrambles to find a hero at almost any opportunity, it amazes me when I read my father's scrapbooks from his glory days to see what some of the supposed 'experts' thought of the man who was so greatly worshipped in France, Italy and even New Caledonia—some of what they say is downright disgraceful. I've learned how well loved Dad was in those foreign lands from first-hand experience. At the beginning of the year 2000, for instance, I was having a hot chocolate at one of my favourite hang-outs, the Spy Cafe in downtown Sydney, and was introduced to some Argentinians. When they heard my father is Tony 'Moondini' they produced their cameras and photographed me in a boxer's stance to show their pals back in South America. I have also read that such was his status throughout the Pacific ports that once, after he had a drink of cola in a milk bar, the Noumean shop owner displayed the bottle in his front window with a sign proclaiming: 'Tony Mundine drank from this bottle—it will be on sale on Monday for 40,000 Pacific Francs'.

Thankfully Dad now receives the accolades he deserved. They might be twenty years too late, but these days he's given a healthy round of applause wherever he goes. But during his glory days he endured some of the worst criticism ever dished out to any Australian athlete, despite boasting a career record which stands tall alongside the likes of Les Darcy, Vic Patrick, Jack Carroll, Jeff Fenech and Jeff Harding. My father's career highlights included locking horns with the great middleweight Carlos Monzon when there was only one world title; winning the Commonwealth championship in *two* weight divisions; flooring the great Emille Griffiths in Paris; and having the legendary boxing trainer Ern McQuillan rate him higher than the great Dave Sands. Yet to scan my father's scrapbooks is to read derogatory comments from the likes of Mike Gibson. His last comment on Tony Mundine's career was downright insulting.

Call it a glass jaw, call it a disinclination to absorb pain or whatever you like, but the world title prospects of a fighter carrying such a glaring weakness in his armoury rank with those of a haemophiliac who aspires to win an Olympic gold medal at fencing. The other night, 30 years of age, 12 years after embarking on his fistic career and without his old

mentor Ern McQuillan from whom he has since parted, Tony got knocked out again. This time it was in Surfers' Paradise in three rounds, by a light-heavyweight called Yacqui Lopez. I watched on television as Tony slumped to the canvas and assumed the horizontal pose, dazed and confused as the referee counted him out. I think that's what saddens me most about Tony Mundine today. The sheer futility of it all, the folly of a good bloke who still believes he can win a world title.
*The Bulletin*, 15 December 1981, p. 106

Reading that type of rubbish makes me fume, man, but my father's advice has always stayed with me. He's long said of his critics that they didn't know the difference between a drop kick and a left hook. And it's funny, because at the stage of life I'm now at, I sometimes hear myself say the same type of thing when Dad and Mum are upset by a poison pen headline about me.

When I was a boy Dad told me his only expectations for me were that I became a nice guy. He wanted me to respect my elders, look after my body and to bite my tongue if I felt the urge to cuss. Once I used a four-letter word, and the whacks I received from Dad's beefy hands ensured I never uttered such a thing in his or Mum's presence again. I think Dad has always realised that as the head of a family the father sets the standard for the kids to follow.

I have found him to be humble, and a man who gets a great deal of satisfaction from helping people in need. One time, when I was about eleven, he was hailed as the hero of Eveleigh Street by an Asian lady when he got back $10,000 cash stolen by two young dudes who ran into a terrace house. My father dragged them around the back alley and 'recovered' the money. He gave it to the grateful lady, a hairdresser, and she told the newspaper, 'For a good man like Tony, haircuts are free in my place.'

He's always been like that, putting himself out for strangers. Despite his immense success Dad never forgot the plight of the Aborigines and he's used his clout to try to raise people out of the gutter. His efforts were rewarded in 1986 when his work for the Aboriginal community earned him the Order of Australia medal. But while I have grown up hearing strangers tell him what he means to them, I've never really told my father how much I love him, and that's wrong because I could not have been blessed with a greater role model. While he and Mum have been separated for sixteen years, he has never neglected his responsibilities as a father or as a man. It is my dream to one day repay him for his faith and support, and I guess the first step I can take to achieve that is to say: I love you, Dad. You freak me out!

In 1996, when I turned twenty-one, I signed with the Broncos. There was a lot more to that decision than wanting to play alongside Allan Langer, Wendell Sailor, Glenn Lazarus and Steve Renouf. I did it for my mum. I was well aware that she longed to live beneath the Queensland sun. She thought of Brisbane as having an ideal lifestyle, and she also had family there. At that stage of her life Mum needed a change and I was happy to be able to help her. I'll long remember how happy she was when I told her we were heading north. It made everything well worthwhile.

She is a tremendous supporter too—number one. In 1999, for instance, when I made public my thoughts on the Australian Rugby League's team selection policy and how it discriminated against Aborigines such as David Peachey, Nathan Blacklock and myself, Mum stood by me when people I really counted on for support turned away and left me hanging. Rather than hide,

Mum told the media: 'I know Anthony speaks from the heart. I'm not sure whether it's the colour of their skin but they have certainly proven themselves on the field this year. They don't know what more they have to do.'

While Dad has been the role model for me to follow, Mum has been the backbone of our family for as long as I can recall. I can't get by without her. And while I have a nice place by the beach in beautiful Cronulla, I can't stay away from home and Mum's love and support. It's priceless, cuz.

# CHAPTER 2

# BROTHER SOLOMON AND CO.

*I don't have a blood brother, but if I could choose one it would be Anthony...*
Solomon Haumono on the ties that bind, 1998

O ne of the great assets I still have from my infant years is a bunch of loyal mates who've stood right beside me in the good—and bad—times of my career and life. We're a tight mob, they're my A-team. Among them is Steve Brown, a white kid I've known since kindergarten, and mighty Solomon Haumono, who I've known since we were babes in nappies when we played together while our fathers did their boxing training at old Ernie McQuillan's gym in Wilson Street, Newtown. And then there's the gang: Wes Patten, Barry Boyd, Lindsay 'Munk' Munroe Abs and Freddie 'G'. The majority of them are either of Aboriginal or Pacific Islander descent and as kids we did the normal things kids do—played sport, went to the movies and chased girls. It was pretty innocent stuff and I remember those times fondly.

It didn't surprise too many people who know Solomon and me that he took up boxing at the same time as I did, because we're soul brothers. We've been through plenty together and our journey into the boxing world is yet another of our lives' adventures.

Solomon is a special pal. As we grew, so too did our friendship. We're so tight we could be related by blood and I can't think of too many friendships which are as pure as the one we

10

enjoy. We've looked out for one another since we were kids, and I have a strong feeling we always will. He is a man of many talents. It seems a contradiction to me that one of the most explosive forwards to ever play Rugby League is also a talented artist who finished Higher School Certificate art with the kind of marks Claude Monet would have been proud of. Solomon is a special guy blessed with numerous other qualities, not least his loyalty and capacity for love. He's a good guy to have watch your back because I know he'd be the last person to desert you when the chips are down and the bad guys are hunting you. He is a very spiritual person who puts those he loves before himself. I find him a joy to be around because he has no cynicism. He's refused to allow bitterness to cloud his vision, even though there have been a few challenges in his life which would have destroyed most other men—especially his well-publicised romance, and then breakup, with the cover girl Gabrielle Richens.

As I have said, big Solomon is the kind of guy who gives his heart and soul to someone, and when Gabrielle returned to England while he played for Canterbury, he missed her terribly. Those feelings, I reckon, were intensified by his disappointing season at Belmore. You see, despite being picked for the Super League Australian and New South Wales teams, Solomon felt as if his career was heading nowhere. He didn't feel fulfilled. The Canterbury hierarchy did very little for his feelings of self-worth when they leaked a story to the *Sydney Morning Herald*. They said that Solomon was forbidden to have a mobile phone because he didn't pay the bills; they said he had to work in the football office from 9 a.m. to 5 p.m. so they could keep an eye on him.

All in all, they painted a portrait of a man incapable of looking after his own welfare. Not only was it extremely insulting, but it was also the straw that broke the camel's back. Solomon had had enough and decided to make a midnight flight to England to see Gabrielle. It was such a spur of the moment decision he didn't even pack a bag. And he risked a $200,000 contract. His decision created plenty of controversy and, in the light of all the questions being asked of him, I decided to hop on a flight to England in an attempt to straighten things out. I had no doubt Solomon could look after himself, but I was worried for him.

Thankfully when Solomon dashed to England the Dragons had a bye. That meant I could launch what was dubbed by the media a 'rescue' mission. While some people at St George—especially Johnny Raper—didn't like the idea of me going to England, I worked out a timetable which would allow me to be back at Kogarah Oval in time for our Thursday afternoon training. It was tight, and it was a drain—but I figured Solomon needed me. I boarded flight QF001 Sydney–Bangkok–London at 4.46 p.m. and arrived in the northern hemisphere twenty-three hours later. While I watched the inflight movie my thoughts often drifted to what big Solomon meant to me and in my heart-of-hearts I knew I was doing the right thing. Indeed, saving Sol was on my mind when I prepared to clear customs. I'd told the press corps I'd bring my brother home, and they were treating it with all the gravity of an SAS mission. 'I'm going to be in, I'm going to be out,' I vowed. 'I'm going to bring back my brother Solomon . . . I'm deeply concerned about Solomon—he hasn't done something like this before and I know he needs me. He was very upset really, especially after people said he was having psychiatric help and things like that.'

When I located Solomon in England I could tell he was happy and at peace. But once he saw me and we had spoken about his situation on the other side of the world, he realised he had no choice but to return to Sydney and sort things out.

Solomon's flight for romance was big news in Australia, and he was called plenty of things—including football's answer to Romeo!

On our touchdown in Sydney we were warned by airline officials and customs that there was a huge media contingent waiting for us in the terminal. I could see the trepidation in Solomon's eyes, and I tried to perk him up by saying luck might have it that Canterbury would react to what he'd done by tearing up his contract thereby opening the way for him to link up with me at Kogarah. (It didn't.) While customs gave us the kind of special clearance they afford VIPs, we couldn't avoid the media scrum. Man, those dudes with cameras and microphones were onto him like hounds on a fox. There was no escape. They harassed him all the way to the limo we had waiting with its engine running. To be honest I was terribly jet-lagged and weary, but I was also overjoyed at knowing my mission was a great success. Solomon was safely home and I figured everything would settle down and sort itself out.

It didn't. I heard St George stalwart Johnny Raper was critical of my decision to use our bye to fly to the other side of the globe and retrieve a brother who had a mind full of problems. He thought I should have stayed in Sydney. But I maintained that the way I chose to spend my time off was not his concern and so I opened up what was to become a verbal barrage by calling him a 'yesterday's man' and 'heartless'. Even now Raper's reaction riles me because it seems, if I was so inclined, I could have stayed in Sydney and drunk myself stupid all weekend. Because of the way Rugby League culture is, that most likely wouldn't have been a problem for him.

Solomon survived the drama but his contract with Canterbury didn't. Nor did his relationship with Gabrielle. He joined Balmain for the '99 season a single man, and there were high hopes he'd add some extra crunch to Wayne Pearce's side but injuries hammered him from the outset. When he was released for the 2000 season I was onto the Dragons like a rocket for them to recruit my brother. I figured he had the power and class to help us go that extra step and win a premiership. But after a committed start Solomon's passion began to wane.

I had held high expectations for him, and his decision to leave the club disappointed me deeply. However, I have only recently appreciated it was wrong for me to lay that trip on Solomon. While I thought it would be his season of all seasons, Solomon had a greater need to come to terms with himself and what he wanted to do with his life. After weeks of contemplating his life's cause, Solomon advised the Dragons' players and coaching staff that he wanted to retire so he could pursue his religious studies. The Dragons, especially coach David Waite and chief executive Brian Johnston, accepted his decision. Even though I'd fought on his behalf for a contract, I realise it was up to him to decide how far he wanted to go.

Solomon made a brief return to the Dragons, but after languishing in First Division he concluded his heart wasn't in football, and he left the place without so much as a goodbye.

This second time I could understand why he left and it has helped us become even closer. Solo is 'The Man's man' and he knows where he sits in my life. He's at the right hand, brother.

# BELIEFS

# CHAPTER 3

# EDUCATION EQUALS LIBERATION

*What's the sense of trying to pass the Intermediate. Will that get me a sharper pick?*

An Aboriginal boy's response to a Sydney Morning Herald journalist's question on education—
20 August 1966

Sport has long been an important part of my life, but from an early age it was drummed into my head by Mum and Dad that education should be my priority. While I was far from the greatest scholar, I did my best at school and worked overtime to get my Higher School Certificate because I realised that piece of paper is the key to *everyone's* future in these highly competitive times. Take it from me, if you want to be a 'something' in the real world you need that certificate, and whenever I visit schools around the country I push that as hard as possible. I believe there are many intelligent Aboriginal kids but it's a fact that they aren't motivated—or pushed—enough to excel in the classroom. However, it's crucial we change this because knowledge is power, and it's the power of the mind which is going to eventually liberate the Aboriginal people from their lowly status in Australia.

You see, becoming educated is a two-pronged process. First and foremost, in a country like Australia education is as much a right as it is a privilege. Second, you have to justify that right by working hard. No matter what you want to do with your life, there's no doubt you'll be at a severe disadvantage if you leave school unable to spell or add up. It has long been my vision to encourage Aboriginal children to pursue their education. As a former top grade footballer with world boxing title aspirations I tell kids the Aboriginal race doesn't need more athletes; we need professionals in the medical, engineering, legal and other fields. The black Americans realised this in the 1960s, and forty years on they have top professionals who help give African–Americans a much stronger voice both politically and socially.

The Aboriginal attitude towards education seems to be slowly, but surely, changing. I must admit I had goose bumps when I heard of the amazing determination of an eighteen-year-old Aboriginal girl from Wilcannia who, in 1999, became the first child—black or white—to gain the Higher School Certificate in the New South Wales town's 105-year history! Wilcannia is infamous for riots, petrol sniffing, soaring unemployment, droughts and other dramas, but in what can best be described as an against-the-odds effort, Heidi Bugmy broke the drought—and how. Indeed, New South Wales Premier Bob Carr made special mention of the hardships she overcame when he singled her out for a special award. While city kids take teachers and computers for granted, many of Heidi's lessons were conducted via the fax machine and telephone because the 160-kilometre distance to the nearest 'big' school, in Menindee, made it difficult for her to have much contact with schoolteachers and other Year 12 pupils. I'm well aware some people will dismiss Heidi's achievement as no big deal. But I think it's great to know her effort to see that final year through has inspired three other kids to give the HSC their best shot. The trio includes her younger sister, a twenty-four year old and a nineteen year old with a baby. It's magic stuff, and I hope this is one trend which continues.

Now that we're at the dawn of the 21st century, Aboriginal

kids must understand the benefits of education. Nevertheless, while I learnt plenty from hitting the books, one of my earliest lessons in Canterbury South Public School's playground was my awareness of being different to most of the other kids. Many of them would let me know this too. I was called things like 'piccaninny' and 'Abo'. My race didn't become an issue until I turned nine and I can only hazard a guess that that's the age when we're no longer 'colour blind'. We realise our mates are fat, redheaded, Asian, Middle Eastern or Aboriginal. Maybe that's when the innocence starts to die. Perhaps they hear their parents say something—a few of the kids would make wise-cracks about witchetty grubs for breakfast and boomerangs not coming back. Such insults would upset me, but unlike the Olympic hurdler Kyle Van der Krup who responded to similar taunts by trying to scratch the blackness from his skin, *I* fired up, and took my antagonists on. There were times when the kids who dared insult me because of my skin ended up being punched on the nose, encounters which normally ended with an angry teacher rushing in to stop the violence. I quickly found there is a real truth in the unwritten rule that might is right, because the insults stopped dead when the kids realised I could—*and would*—use my fists. These days I believe violence achieves very little. However, it is important you understand that back then it was one kid against a mob of young fools and in such times my fists were my best allies.

Other lessons weren't so straightforward because the system I was brought up in rewarded the pupils who could best regurgitate the teacher's words. The so-called smart kids didn't appear too big on initiative or asking questions. Instead they just jotted down what the teacher said and accepted it as gospel. It was also very frustrating to be taught Aboriginal Studies by a non-Aboriginal person; there were questions I asked which couldn't be answered because they weren't in the textbook. The teacher would give a blank look and ramble on about traditional Aboriginal art and didgeridoos. Obviously I would have liked a greater emphasis placed on Aboriginal studies. I would have loved to have gone on an excursion to the outback to meet with the elders. It would have been great at an early age to have seen the true dignity of the Aboriginal warriors. However, you have to deal with situations as they are, so I spent plenty of time trawling the Internet and bang, bang, bang my big brown eyes were opened to the plight of my people. I became absorbed by all the issues I have been campaigning about since I made a name for myself with the Dragons and Brisbane. It's strange, but when you think about it, my Aboriginal studies teacher's ignorance actually helped make me an Aboriginal campaigner!

# CHAPTER 4

# HUMAN REFUSE

*I respect him. He's a good boy. He doesn't smoke, he doesn't drink, he doesn't swear. He's involved in sport. Yeah, he gets a lot of publicity. But that doesn't change the fact that he's a nice young boy and that there are a lot of good things in his life.*
Tony Mundine on his son, the Sunday Telegraph, 1999

R unning from the terrace house and into the darkness of the backstreets which form mazes around the high density Housing Commission area of Waterloo, I felt a terrible fear and a pain in my heart. I was only a teenager and had just been offered hard drugs by someone I considered a good friend and it freaked me out. While I felt no temptation to join him in his indulgence, I did feel as if I had done something wrong by being in a position where I was asked if I wanted to try drugs. I now know this was really an invitation to be yet *another* black face among the growing drug culture. I'd trusted the person, I thought he was OK, but I was wrong. I wandered around the streets feeling lost and confused; I held my head in my hands and asked myself, Why? Why? Why? And then, not for the first time in my life, I started bawling like a baby at the futility of the drug scene and for the people I know who've lost themselves because of it. All I could think to myself was not to cry anymore. 'Don't cry, Chocy baby,' I told myself, 'because one day you're going to be someone; you're going to be something. But you gotta be stronger than the rest of them and you have to sidestep

21

the weaklings who'll drag you down with them and drown you.'
With all that racing about in my head—the hurt, the anger, the
confusion—I told myself I was a good kid and I'd be rewarded
one day for staying straight.

There were other opportunities for me to go down the
wrong path in life. I could have joined inner city gangs, taken
part in street fights or a host of other bad things. However, I'd
set my course from a young age and a long stretch in prison
wasn't a part of it. I developed tunnel vision in my pursuit of
excellence and the idea of success drove me. As someone who
has never partaken of drugs, including tobacco and alcohol, I
don't understand why people let those substances get a grip on
them until it chokes the life out of them. I've had a friend staying at my place for quite a while because she's been fighting her
heroin addiction. I know her father and he's a good bloke.
However, his daughter's problems became too much and after
being tested once too often he showed her the door. As a friend
I could not let her just wander about Kings Cross and risk
becoming yet another statistic. I was well aware of the risks I
took when I opened the door to her; I knew the day might
come when I returned home to find my television or video had
been pawned because she needed some quick money. But it
doesn't scare me. And I won't give up on her, because it is a
battle which must be won.

As for alcohol, which has long been a part of Australian culture, I think the first thing we have to do is convince our role
models—the athletes, actors and so on—to be more responsible. I don't know how many of those pen pics our footballers
do, and every time they're asked what their favourite drink is
they fire back that it's some form of alcohol. Why can't they
nominate fruit juice or water, or some other soft drink? It also
annoys me that whenever sportspeople do something special,

like win a grand final, the first thing they do is reach for a beer or shower themselves in champagne. They don't realise that kids watch everything they do and what they are saying to them is, hey, you can equate good times with alcohol.

As for the Aborigine and alcohol, well, the truth is the white man introduced it to us. When the first black was offered a swig of wine from the European settlers, he spat it out because the taste was so vile. However, in time, when the Aborigines learned they could enter a different stratosphere by becoming intoxicated, alcohol became mother's milk for too many of them. It has stopped them from progressing, from becoming somebody. I know many white Australians like to think of my race as people who lie under trees drinking their life away. But they should remember that before their ancestors arrived from Europe my people had never drunk grog. When the whites realised us blacks could not handle it, the demon water became a form of control.

My father put me on the right path when I was a kid. He made it painfully clear that he'd show no mercy if he ever caught me taking drugs, drinking alcohol or smoking cigarettes. When I was a boy Dad would reinforce how dangerous those vices could be by taking me to Kings Cross to show me how addictions had ruined some street kids' lives before they'd even started really living. Sometimes, when we'd drive along William Street, I'd peer into the shadows and see the faceless hordes of homeless kids selling their bodies for the price of a quick fix. I would hear Dad whisper his rage, 'It disgusts me . . . it disgusts me, Choc, to see all these beautiful girls and boys being used and abused.'

Dad's message was tattooed on my brain. Whenever in later years I was offered a sneaky swig of alcohol by a mate or a puff of marijuana, I refused. Not only did I not want to run the risk of becoming like them, but I also didn't want to disappoint the greatest man I know.

Unfortunately, drugs are a real problem in Australia and it saddens me to think this country has one of the worst reputations in the world for drug usage. Rugby League officials took commendable steps to stamp out the drug menace from the game after it was revealed that some misguided players were using their profiles as football stars to sell drugs to starry-eyed kids.

However, I am adamant the grog problem is just as bad and I'm afraid it too will be part of Australian society so long as we continue to place what can only be described as an unhealthy emphasis on the so-called pleasures of getting drunk. We glamorise alcohol and, for reasons I can't understand, there's a perception that unless a man—or woman—gets plastered and makes a gibbering fool of themselves they've had a tame night. Believe me, that attitude certainly exists in the League; it's not an after-match function unless there is a trough of alcohol available for the players' consumption. In some instances it seems as if a new player's initiation into the team isn't giving blood on the field but drinking until he vomits. I've sidestepped it. I can't see the need for it. When kids hear international footballers carrying on about the virtues of grog, well, it sets a dangerous example. If I were in charge of the NRL, I would request players refrain from nominating any alcoholic beverage as their favourite drink in the pen pics. They're seen by thousands of kids. Alcohol companies aren't allowed to advertise during children's television time slots so why should we push their products in articles read by kids? Why a footballer chooses to associate himself with a particular brand of alcohol is beyond me. Some blokes treat requests to endorse a charity as being akin to having their teeth pulled. Yet they're quick to give a particular brand of demon water a free plug in the media.

What also amazes me about the grog culture is that while most football supporters are aware I'm a teetotaller they still try to ply me with drinks. It seems to be some sort of challenge. But they're wasting their time. No poison is going to pass my lips.

While I have abstained from boozy nights, other players have dived into the scene headfirst. They may as well be swimming in a pool full of man-eating sharks. While I don't approve, I'm not too judgmental because, unlike outsiders, I realise the pressure on young players to drink from an early age is intense. Many youngsters cave in because they're weak. Unfortunately they think getting drunk with the senior stars will mean an automatic acceptance, and that's wrong. I don't believe anyone can be themselves when they take a mind-altering substance, legal or otherwise.

Because I'm well aware of the unofficial Rugby League powerbase—the bar-room—I sympathise with the likes of North Queensland's Julian O'Neill. Julian has created plenty of bad headlines via his drunken escapades, including his 1999 efforts in the Dubbo motel where he and some Souths players trashed a room. However, I maintain he's been a victim of the football environment—and that means drink. I really feel for him, because, while he's a nice enough bloke, Julian has had a genuine problem. Knowing that, I find it hard when I hear some people label him bad news, especially when there *are* some arrogant, pigheaded blokes who think they're immune from any responsibility because of their profile.

As a first grade footballer I have been offered drugs from time to time, but because of the way I was brought up I'm not tempted in any shape or form. I've seen the empty shells of people who've fallen victim to the white powder and nasty green leaf. Look, drugs kill. You have to be a fool to tempt fate by popping a tablet or sticking a needle in your veins. Junkies say they clog their arteries with chemicals because it helps them chill; they supposedly enter a new dimension and escape their problems. The truth is, they're selfish, because with each hit they break the hearts of their parents, brothers, sisters, aunts, uncles, cousins, friends and, in some cases, their kids. I can't understand how this can be seen as a glamorous or exciting life. The Man gets high on life and the drug that brings that state of mind, brother, is the power of positive thought—and you don't have to be famous or wealthy to attain that. You get it from appreciating the simple things in life, like watching a sunset or going for a good run.

The emergence of the big money in professional Rugby League has also meant that many players are looking for an edge—and for some that has come in the form of steroids. It's pathetic and says nothing at all for their strength of character. If a player needs steroids to compete at the elite level, he shouldn't be there. I am driven by success; I'm constantly re-setting my goals and aspirations but if I had to rely on an outside boost from steroids I'd hang up my boots and go fishing down the local creek. I rely instead upon my adrenalin, my pride and my natural skills to get me to the top. I don't cheat—and I have no tolerance for those who do.

# CHAPTER 5

# LEAP OF FAITH

*I believe there is one God and you have to believe in that God. And you have to believe He has a message for the people. It is a really peaceful religion and I have an inner peace now. I have a different look on life.*
*My description to the media of my conversion to Islam, February 1999*

I have always believed in a divine creator but, until I spent three years studying the Holy Koran and the teachings of the Islam prophets, I did not know His name was Allah. *Allah be praised!* When I was a child my parents had me baptised Church of England, and while my family believed in God they weren't what you'd call overly religious. We only went to church on rare occasions and I can't really recall too many religious discussions at the kitchen table. However, I was raised to respect my fellow humans and to treat others as I'd expect them to treat me. As an adult I rejected the ways of Christianity because I had trouble grasping the concept of the Holy Trinity. I couldn't accept God was in His heavenly kingdom and also on earth in the form of Jesus. I also don't believe Jesus died for the sins of humankind because, as Muslims, we believe God is all forgiving. Even so we're taught that every man, woman and child is responsible for their own actions, and they must suffer the consequences if they continue to cross the line south of righteousness.

However, what people don't realise is that Islam and Christianity are very similar. While we Muslims reject the notion that Jesus was God, we do believe he existed as a prophet. Indeed, he's one of the greatest messengers. Nonetheless, another reason I rejected Christianity was because I cannot believe that the Christians who started and staffed the Aboriginal missions in the outback believed in the same god as me. I don't doubt some of the priests and nuns who were dispatched to the outback to save some supposed 'black' (as in sinful) souls went with good intentions. But there were a great many who acted like barbarians. I'm certain they'll have plenty to answer for come judgment day. You see, while we live by the idea all people are born equal, many members of the stolen generations were made to feel bad about the colour of their skin by religious people. One woman was placed in a home that had a big poster showing Aboriginal people at the end of a road, playing cards, gambling and drinking, with the slogan, 'Wide is the road that leads us to destruction, which leads up into hell.' Another 'survivor' from Western Australia has never forgotten the sexual abuse he suffered at the hands of the Christian Brothers in the 1940s.

The missionaries didn't allow others to speak their native language, calling it the 'devil's tongue'. They'd use soap to wash out the mouth of anyone who dared utter it. Ultimately, forcing the children to adopt the language of the Bible helped to kill off the Aboriginal dialects in the areas they 'civilised'.

I am well aware some people believe I only embraced Islam because it is the religion of Muhammad Ali and Malcolm X, but that's ridiculous. While it is true I have been influenced by Ali's efforts to lift his people's self-esteem and status in society, I'd be a fool to follow such things as his religious preference blindly. My decision to embrace Islam followed three solid years of study and discussions with committed Muslims. To be honest, my decision to convert was not initially welcomed by my father because he was worried by two things: first, the perception promoted by the Western press that all

Muslims are murderous terrorists; and, second, the fear that I was going to have the money I had earned ripped off. However, once I explained to Dad that it was a spiritual thing, and not about money (I told him I only intended to help poor people) he was 'sweet'.

Islam is the world's fastest growing religion, brother, and I think big Solomon, who converted with me, best explained the way we felt when he told the press he felt as if he'd just come out of his mother's womb—it was that powerful feeling of being blessed and born again.

> This is a very strong experience. My mind has been broadened and I have a whole new meaning to life. People relate being Muslim to being a terrorist. That's because they have tunnel vision. I had that as well. My views are very different now. I will be doing my best to keep the faith. I will not be drinking, smoking and pre-marital sex is also out. Sex between two people is a very special thing. Today's society is all sex, sex, sex. It's not right. I have not had sex since the day I converted and I am aiming to keep my faith.

When I accepted Islam into my life I was told honouring Allah was much more than paying lip service. Here's what Solomon and I are expected to do to be good Muslims.

> **Pray five times daily**
> **Eat only halal meat**
> **Visit Mecca**
> **Refrain from eating pork**
> **Abstain from alcohol, tobacco and drugs**
> **Only have sex with legal wife**

You'll realise that it isn't an easy road to follow. But what I like best about my religion is everyone is seen as being equal in Allah's eyes. The only way a fellow Muslim can be better than me is if they are closer to God—and that is a question of spirituality and righteousness. I'm trying hard to be righteous and while I don't drink, smoke or take drugs, and try not to speak ill of people, there is a lot more to it than that. I'm sure Cronulla Sharks prop Jason Stevens, a committed Christian and good friend of mine, would agree Western society makes it hard to follow a virtuous life. However, I see myself as more fortunate than the non-believers because *this* is their paradise and it doesn't get any better for them than what they have.

I'm striving for paradise and to get there I have adopted a humble lifestyle. While most people worship the trappings of materialism, I have rejected them. God has given us all the faculty of reasoning and how as a species have we reacted? We've built a system on the foundations of wealth, greed, oppression and power. Perhaps the most immediate example I can offer of a Muslim who turned his back on the trappings of Western success when he realised it didn't offer him spiritual fulfilment is the 1970s pop star, Cat Stevens. One day he realised his lyrics left people in a state of depression because they were about broken hearts and lost spirits. He walked away from his previous lifestyle, and he hasn't looked back.

Because of my upbringing I try to be humble. I am humble. I like to meet people and I try to spread my love. When I meet someone I'm not scared to put my arm around them as a sign of peace, and I travel by public transport a few times a week so people can talk to me. If they want to bag me and say they think I'm a fool, well, that's cool. If they meet me and see me for what I really am—and that's no better or worse than them—then that's great. Such is the perceived status of athletes, however, most people just ask what the heck I'm doing travelling on the public network! I say, 'The same as you bro, I'm getting to point B.'

One thing about Islam is that it makes it crystal clear everyone is accountable not only for their own actions, but also their religious education. It is up to each person to find solutions to their questions by reading the Koran. That means I can't rely on someone else to tell me how Allah wants us to live our lives, because that person may have misinterpreted the readings or corrupted them for their own reasons. I believe God has given us our two eyes, a brain and the faculty of reasoning to find the truth for ourselves, and I'm trying to do that. Islam has made me a stronger person. I fear nothing and no-one. The Muslim practice of Ramadan at the height of summer during pre-season training is a true test. We aren't allowed to consume food or beverages during the daylight hours and I missed training on a few occasions because I was struck down by a mystery virus. To St George's credit, the hierarchy and my team-mates accepted my decision to fast, even though they asked plenty of questions. The Dragons' dietitian helped me hydrate myself by advising me to eat plenty of fruit and vegetables and to drink plenty of fluid when the sun sank over the western skies.

I have long realised there are people sweating on seeing people like Solomon and me slip up, and that was no better reflected than when Solo retired from the Dragons to find himself. Before St George-Illawarra even kicked a ball in anger in the Year 2000 premiership he was photographed having lunch during Ramadan. The media questioned his faith, but what the journalists didn't realise was under the rules of Ramadan a Muslim is allowed to break the fast if he is sick or travelling. Solo was ill with influenza when that (cheap) shot was taken.

Ramadan is designed to strengthen the spirit, not weaken the body. Ramadan teaches us to control our emotions when we're hungry, to keep our moods in check and to stay in tune with Allah, because he's in our thoughts when we waver and consider having a drink. Ramadan helps us to appreciate the things we take for granted—like food and water. It also encourages compassion because at the end of it each Muslim has to donate money to someone close to them who is experiencing financial hardship.

I am dedicated to the Muslim cause and I considered it a great honour the night I was asked to lead the prayers at a friend's barbecue, because normally the man to lead the prayers is the most knowledgeable. Part of my duty as a Muslim is to one day visit Mecca and the thought that I'll experience there the love and fellowship of brothers from all over the world excites me. Indeed, it makes me proud to think that when my conversion became public knowledge at least ten Aborigines in the maximum security wing of Sydney's Long Bay prison followed my example and embraced Islam. And it makes me glad knowing God's love will help them become better people. It is my plan to contact each of them and help strengthen their resolve to live the right life. In fact, it is my firm belief that until there is a true brotherhood and sisterhood among Aborigines— and it is lacking at the moment—we won't move forward; we'll always be on the back foot.

With God's help my aim is to better myself and to keep trying to meet the challenges thrown up at me in the form of desire. And it's hard, but His help will steel my resolve.

# MY PEOPLE

# CHAPTER 6

# DECLARATION OF WAR

*I wish the kid good luck; he's talked the talk, now he's got to go out and walk it...*

*Former World Champion boxer Jeff Fenech after my Eveleigh Street press conference, 5 May 2000*

T he rain was pelting down when I entered the Eveleigh Street gymnasium named after my father. But that downpour was nothing compared to the storm my answers to some probing questions were about to unleash around the country. As a friend put it, I did the next best thing to declaring war on society. My views, such as that the Aboriginal man has to stop thinking what the white man has taught him, made white Australia shift uncomfortably in its seat.

I'd invited the media en masse to my turf, Redfern, so they could hear why I'd abandoned a lucrative Rugby League contract midway through the 2000 season to pursue the uncertainty of a boxing career in the super-middleweight division. But I was going to take the opportunity to offer my opinions on the way John Howard is running the nation. Such was the public interest in a bloke who turned his back on a $600,000-a-year deal, an army of journalists turned up with microphones, television cameras and the occasional tough question. I was psyched for a grilling.

However, something that warmed me on my arrival at the gymnasium was the number of Aborigines who turned out in a show of support. Their brotherly love, especially that of the

Eveleigh Street kids, gave me a tremendous strength. So I figured I was putting myself on the line for their future. I believe I can help make a difference for them in—and out of—the ring. Plenty of Aborigines, such as my dad, Ron Richards, Jack Hassen, Lionel Rose, Hector Thompson and the Kelly brothers have given our race a tremendous sense of pride with their feats in the boxing ring. I want to take it a step further. I want Aborigines to look at me and realise we all really have a power of one within us. It was always my belief that when the bell sounded for me to come out of the corner for my first bout I'd put everything on the line to push that.

However, I realise it's going to take some tough words to stir my brothers, and that was why I prepared myself for the 'worst case scenario' questions the press might have asked. One thing which *really* disappointed me was seeing that my old media foes—*and they know who they are*—weren't among the sea of faces. Maybe they realised the heat from my kitchen would be far too hot, so they kept well away. Even though they weren't there I realised it was important to retain control over the proceedings, so from the outset I requested that each person asking a question not only identify themselves but also state the news organisation they worked for. After setting out these guidelines I told the press my reasons for turning my back on Rugby League were threefold:

**(1) The level of racism entrenched in the game**
**(2) My belief that I'd accomplished everything an outspoken young Aborigine could achieve in Rugby League**
**(3) My desire to box**

Within a split second of the last of my opening words—which was to say being Aboriginal and outspoken isn't a good mixture—the press started firing their questions. The day before the conference I was advised by a few people not to burn my bridges with the Rugby League world because, they reasoned, I might one day want to return. I appreciated the tip, but the way I viewed my situation was that I had a captive media audience and I wanted to make each word—each point—count. I wanted to awaken others to the plight of my people, and to do that I realised I not only had to risk burning bridges, but be prepared to blow up the entire city. That, I figured, was the only way I could make my point. Also, while I had said in the lead up to my press conference that there was a chance I might one day return to Rugby League, I'm now fully focused on and determined to make it in boxing. That super-middleweight world title is my quest and I intend to do something constructive along the way to winning it. Even so, I know people will try to obstruct my path. They want to see me get cut up, hurt and humiliated. Some cynics want to see my pretty face get mashed. Indeed, two faxes I carried in my breast pocket during the press conference were reminders of the hatred and the ignorance I'll oppose. One was a media release from One Nation's David Oldfield and the other was allegedly from a former St George prop. I won't identify the man, or the company letterhead on which the message appeared, because it wasn't signed. However, if the words— that I am, among other things, a 'little prick'—are the alleged old Dragon's true feelings, then I wouldn't mind talking to him like a man, and face to face.

Yeah, the two faxes fuelled my desire to make a stand because they were tainted with the dreadful stains of racism and ignorance. See for yourself.

Oldfield's said:

# THE MAN

### 'THE MAN is just acting like a boy'

So what if Anthony Mundine gives up a $600,000 salary and never plays football again, no doubt there are many talented young Australians just itching to take his place. We should not overplay the importance of this situation—ultimately, be it good or bad, it will only affect a few Mundines, no-one else.

I've never met Anthony Mundine so in fairness I can't be too judgmental but it occurs to me that anyone who so consistently and publicly calls themselves 'THE', anything, be it man, be it greatest, be it best, or similar, has a seriously over exaggerated idea of their significance to humankind.

Mundine has shown the Australian selectors to be correct in their evaluation of his lack of suitability to represent Australia, perhaps not only for the reason that there were players better than him, but also because of his irresponsible actions and childish displays of unjustifiable self-importance.

When next Mundine raises the spectre of racism, we should remember it was him who stated that because he was Muslim he had millions of people behind him. I would not support people simply because of their skin colour, religion or similar but because they are right—something Mundine isn't.

In my chosen sport of the time, I once missed out on getting into the NSW team so I joined a team of others who also weren't selected and we beat that NSW team and all the others and won the National Title—while not quite the same avenue might be available to Mundine, the fact is he is a quitter who let down his team and fans.

It's a shame Mundine didn't take the good advice he gave Solomon Haumono when he helped bring him back to Australia. If he now fails to be a champion again, for the rest of his life we'll all hear about how it was because he was

Aboriginal—maybe we should say sorry now just to get it out of the way.

It shouldn't take too much time for you to work out my thoughts on David Oldfield, the party he represents and what it stands for. I believe that, like all politicians, he's a headline seeker. Now that white Australia is starting to wise up to the ugliness of his party he's desperate for publicity. In his misguided wisdom, Oldfield figured he could use me to help get some airspace and his name in the paper. Oldfield, Pauline Hanson and the rest of One Nation are a joke. If you believe they are for fair play and the good of Australia, read that last paragraph of his press release and think again. I have no doubt the colour of my skin—it's black, man—was his biggest problem with me.

The second fax, which I feel inclined to quote fully, was equally as poisonous and pathetic:

This media release is to back up what we have said all along that Anthony Mundine never was much of a footballer and will never amount to anything. If it weren't for our compassion as a club of legends, he would never have played first grade. We would also like to take this opportunity to say that we have never agreed with anything that he has said in the press. Racial discrimination had nothing to do with his non-selection in the Australian Test team, he just can't play the game.

We wish him all the best in his boxing career. He will need all the luck he can get if he is even to win the West Moree flyweight title. Let's hope that some white honky lines him up and knocks the snot out of him. He is probably lucky that Craig Smith is out of his weight division as the big Kiwi would probably knock his block off again if he got the chance.

In moving on we would also like to thank Trent Barrett for his hard work in making the little prick look as good as he has for the last couple of years. Trent will now have the time to make himself look better and perhaps push Freddy [Brad Fittler] out of the five-eighth position in the representative teams.

In closing, we cannot believe that you people have been so naive as to think we actually liked this Anthony at any stage. He is an idiot that will end up going the same way as South Sydney.

There will be no further comment made on this matter.

As you can see, there are people lurking in the shadows waiting to try to trip me up. Most of them are showing their true colours and they're scarlet, as in redneck. They don't phase me, though. If anything, Oldield and the prop helped steel my resolve. Their communications reinforced that all the injustices I have complained about are very real. And, in spite of them, my extended family, close friends, Jeff Fenech, Johnny Lewis, the little kids from Eveleigh Street, the old Aborigines who grew up in an era when it was unsafe for a black to speak out, some St George-Illawarra fans and ex-St George winger Ricky Walford, fronted up to the press conference to hear my views. And they heard me speak up a storm. They listened to my responses to such questions as whether I was running away, to which I replied: 'I've accomplished all I can accomplish for being me. You give me anyone, the immortals (John Raper, Reg Gasnier, Bob Fulton, Clive Churchill, Graeme Langlands and Wally Lewis), anyone at their best, and I'll give them me at my best and they are nothing to me.'

I was also asked how on earth I could accuse the ARL and NRL of being racist when the 1994 Kangaroo tour of Great Britain and France had Aborigines in the team, was captained by a Solomon Islander and had Australians from many other backgrounds playing as well. 'They can put so many in but they turn hundreds away, mate,' I answered.

After saying I thought there were some good people involved in the game, including David Moffett and David Waite, I made the point that some of the 'yesterday's' men had to go because they are out of touch with reality. 'I'm saying most of the people in charge of the game, what era are they from? The '50s and '60s. Aborigines weren't even citizens until 1974. So you tell me where their mentality is at.'

Then, when I was asked why I'd chosen boxing over Rugby League, I made it clear that the square ring was a greater plat-form for me to tell the world of my people's struggle. When Daniel MacDougall of the ABC asked how could I justify my belief that I was the game's best five-eighth when a certain Brad Fittler ruled the ranks, I enjoyed a bit of a verbal spat. 'How can I say it? You been watching the football games over the last five years? You been watching my career? He has never walked off the field against me a winner. Never,' I told him.

'It's more than one game,' MacDougall came back.

'More than one game. Of course it's more than one game. I don't think he's ever beat me in my career, to be honest. I don't think he has. I outshined him every time. I think maybe once he probably had a good game, but every other time I whipped him,' I said.

I went on to make it clear I didn't think Prime Minister John Howard was doing a good job of leading the nation. I stressed how sick and tired I was of my people's portrayal as drug-taking alcoholics who sniff petrol. I told all those journalists—the mainstream media is predominantly white—that they can't under-stand, truly understand, the trials and tribulations of the black man and woman. 'My people are weary of being repressed,' I added.

# THE MAN

Not long after I drove away from Eveleigh Street, I heard the talkback radio hosts and their callers tear shreds off me for being bigmouthed, bigheaded and a big-noter. They couldn't forgive me for my jibe about the immortals and Fittler. That didn't worry me, because even though the sports heads didn't seem to comprehend it, I managed to highlight the Aboriginal cause before a very wide audience. Indeed, I have since been told that had the conference been filmed in black and white it could easily have been mistaken for 1960s footage, when black pride began to surface in the United States and the likes of Malcolm X flexed their muscles. I was happy because that was exactly what I had sought. It's the first step, baby, of a tough marathon. But listen up, my legs are strong and they can carry me over the highest of mountains.

# CHAPTER 7

# WHITE AUSTRALIA HAS A BLACK HISTORY

*You are the new Australians but we are the old Australians . . . We ask only for justice, decency and fair play. Is this too much to ask?*
Open letter from Sydney's Aborigines to white Australia on the 150th Australia Day in 1938

*Australia's treatment of her Aboriginal people will be the thing upon which the rest of the world will judge Australia and the Australians—not just now, but in the greater perspective of history.*
Gough Whitlam, ALP Policy Speech, 1972

Australia Day, the year 2000, and as a nation celebrates its founding and basks beneath the warm summer sun I'm cookin' inside, man. There's a fire blazing so fierce in my heart the steam from my boiling blood brings tears to my eyes. The pain hurts like nothing on earth. While millions of Australians celebrate 'their' national day at backyard barbecues or with re-enactments of Captain Cook's or Arthur Phillip's arrival to *Terra Australis*, I'm consumed by the terrible feeling of emptiness and loneliness that only we, the Aborigines, know. We've lived with it for over 200 years, like a sick person does with their disease. We're downtrodden people and there's a sorrow which weighs on us and it's never any heavier, brother, than on our Survival Day—26 January—a day of Aboriginal mourning.

We've lost our all. Our land, our languages, our customs, even our soul—but if there are any positives to be gleaned as I look down from the stage on Survival Day at thousands of hopeful black faces, it's that we've survived it. And we sing. While thousands of our ancestors were butchered by the white invaders, and while we might be a poor race in an affluent society, I like to think our mere survival is a victory of a kind. On this day the words of people like Anthony Trollope ring in my ears. In 1873 he wrote of my race, 'Of the Australian black man we may certainly say he has to go, that he should perish without unnecessary suffering should be the aim of all who are concerned by the matter.' We defied that train of thought, but I want more than mere survival as a pennant for my race to fly. I want to help lift my people's self-esteem and I want to help change the common perception the wider community has of Aborigines. Indeed, if you listen to what '*they*' say, we are a despondent, disease-ridden race with no sunny future and a primitive, dark past.

The fate of the black people who'd inhabited Australia for 40,000 years before the Europeans first sighted its brilliant shores was determined long before Cook, and then Phillip, set their compasses and followed the stars to the Great South Land. The words of British mariner William Dampier condemned us with his accounts of the Aborigines he encountered during his exploration of north-west Australia in 1688. Take it from me, Dampier sold my ancestors short. Rather than see them as proud warriors he wrote an account which was later used to justify first an invasion and then centuries of murder and rape:

> The inhabitants of this country are the most miserablest in this world. The Hodniadods (Hottentots) of Monomatapa, though a nasty People, yet for wealth are Gentleman to these . . . and setting aside their human shape, they differ but little from brutes. They are tall, strait-bodied, and thin, with small long Limbs. They have great Heads, round Foreheads, and great

Brows. Their eyelids are always half closed to keep Flies out of their Eyes . . . therefore they cannot see far . . . They are long visaged, and of a very unpleasing aspect; having no one graceful feature in their face. They have no house, but lye in the open Air, without any covering, the earth being their bed and the heaven their Canopy . . . the land affords them no food at all. There is neither Herb, Pulse, nor any sort of Grain for them to eat, that we saw, nor any sort of Bird or Beast that they can catch, having no instruments wherewithal to do so. I did not perceive they did worship anything.

Then came that fateful April day in 1770 when James Cook tapped a young midshipman named Isaac Smith on the shoulder as their longboat from the HMS *Endeavour* glided towards the silvery sand at Kurnell. Cook told Smith he would land first. And when that kid leapt into the bottle-green water and waded towards the shore, he shattered forever the barrier which, since the Pleistocene age, had guarded the east coast of this ancient land. Theirs was a brief visit, but life for Australia's original inhabitants was never to be the same. Just eighteen years later, boatloads of chained convicts and red-coated British soldiers stepped from their stinking hulks and ruined the Dreamtime forever by securing an unknown land for a faraway king.

The people Cook encountered were from the Gweagal clan from Kurnell. They are said to have had patterns of scars over their arms and breasts, and many of the men had a bone or stick inserted in a hole through the cartilage of their nose as an ornament, and had had their top right front teeth removed during their initiation into manhood. To his credit, I guess, Cook noted the Europeans could learn a trick or two from their simple way of life. He contradicted Dampier's view when he wrote in his journal:

> They may appear to some to be the most wretched people
> upon Earth, but in reality they are far happier than we Euro-
> peans; being wholly unacquainted not only with the
> superfluous but the necessary Conveniences so much sought
> after in Europe, they are happy in not knowing the use of
> them. They live in Tranquillity which is not disturb'd by the
> Inequity of Condition.

There is a common perception the Aborigine did not defend his land, but that's a lie. Many battles were fought. Even Cook's arrival was confrontational. Unlike in Tahiti, where both English and French boats were greeted by enthusiastic natives, two naked warriors shook their spears in a threatening manner at Cook as his long boat headed to the shore. Cook and the botanist James Banks tried to appease them with offerings of colourful beads and metal nails, but these gifts failed to quieten the pair. Instead they shouted a threat in their native tongue and then made threatening gestures, as if they were ready to attack. Cook fired a round from his 'thunderstick' between them, but rather than retreat, one man ran back to collect a bundle of spears while the other pelted rocks at Cook's boat. Frustrated and angry, the English navigator took aim and wounded one of them with small shot. Even then the warrior didn't scamper into the scrub but simply picked up a full length shield with eye holes in an attempt to protect himself from further injury. In a final effort to drive the whites off they hurled their stone-tipped spears, causing Cook to fire a third shot. The men, realising they were outmatched by a technology they could not fathom, retreated slowly into the woodlands. When the exploration party later came across a number of bark huts, Cook noted his disgust at seeing the adults had left a few babies behind. He asked what kind of people would run and leave their children at the mercy of strangers. I can only hazard a guess they were spooked. There have been some suggestions the Aborigines believed the early whites were ghosts, so maybe they thought the spirits were visiting and it scared them.

After a week Cook was frustrated by the lack of interest the Aborigines showed in him and his crew. *'They seemed to have no curiosity, no sense of material possessions. All they seem'd to want was for us to be gone,'* he wrote. Some historians have suggested that the Aborigines paid a hefty price for not wanting to mix with Cook during his stay. They consider that, when the British needed to establish a penal colony eighteen years later, the memory of a seemingly backward people who reputedly ran from the sight of a white face and who had no property to defend made Australia the perfect dumping ground. It would be a guilt-free conquest. Well, so they thought.

When he was charged with establishing the penal colony of New South Wales, Governor Arthur Phillip's orders were to protect the natives and to punish anyone who harmed them.

Endeavour by every possible means to open an intercourse with the natives, and to conciliate their affections, enjoining all our subjects to live in animity and kindness with them. And if any of our subjects shall wantonly destroy them, or give them any unnecessary interruption in the exercise of their several occupations, it is our will and pleasure that you do cause such offenders to be brought to punishment according to the degree of the offence. You will endeavour to procure an account of the numbers inhabiting the neighbourhood of the intended settlement, and report your opinion to one of our Secretaries of State in what manner our intercourse with these people may be turned to the advantage of this colony.

From all accounts the colonists had no intentions of extermi-
nating or enslaving them. That was to come a few years later
during the great land grab when the grazing and pastoral land
was opened. Then the whites not only poisoned the water, but
gave unsuspecting Aborigines 'gifts' of blankets riddled with the
fatal smallpox germ. The Aborigines suffered not only from
smallpox but also from other diseases the settlers introduced,
and it wasn't uncommon to find the corpses of indigenous
people who had died from the cholera and influenza germs
transferred from the ships to shore.

Phillip *did* protect the Aborigines, but the preferential treatment upset some convicts, who couldn't believe the blacks
would sit higher up the social pecking scale than a white—
albeit a white criminal. One, a Scottish forger named Watling,
wrote:

> Many of these savages are allowed what is termed a freeman's
> ration of provisions for their idleness. They are bedecked at
> times with dress which they make away with [at] the first
> opportunity, preferring the originality of naked nature; and
> they are treated with the most singular tenderness. This you
> will suppose is not more than laudable; but is there one spark
> of humanity exhibited to the poor wretches who are at least
> denominated Christians?

The convicts did nothing to help race relations when they
stole spears and axes to sell to sailors who knew they'd be
worth big money as curios in London. The inconvenience
caused by such thefts meant feeling between the convicts and
Aborigines deteriorated at an alarming rate. A few convicts
were speared on expeditions outside of Port Jackson but
Phillip honoured his orders and refused to send retaliatory

parties out to exact revenge. However, it was a phoney peace. Indeed, despite the handouts and smiles, the first strain between the two cultures surfaced soon after the First Fleet anchored in Botany Bay (before sailing to Sydney Harbour). In what can be described as the first Aboriginal protest, some complained about the Europeans taking too many fish from *their* water and they also protested when the British started cutting down *their* trees.

In a desperate attempt to learn the mysterious ways of the natives, Phillip ordered his troops to kidnap some Aborigines. Before they captured the better-known Bennelong, who was paraded about England like a prize bird, they captured a warrior named Arabanoo at Manly. He was estimated to be aged about thirty and the English were impressed by his hygiene and manner. He not only detested liquor but was repulsed by the floggings and other punishments imposed upon the convicts. Children flocked around him and he was said to have a gentle voice. Unfortunately, he was in Port Jackson when the smallpox epidemic spread through the colony like wildfire, killing many Aborigines, including poor old Arabanoo.

Some historians pinpoint the end of the phoney peace I speak of as 10 December 1790, when a war party killed John McIntire, who hunted animals for Phillip. McIntire's occupation as a hunter not only earned him Aborigines' ire, but he had a reputation for attacking them. His reign of terror ended the fateful night some warriors, led by the future guerilla Pemulwuy, attacked McIntire and the governor's hunting party. McIntire was speared by Pemulwuy, and his act of contrition as he lay dying was to confess to a convict in his party of the terrible crimes he had committed against the Aborigines.

While McIntire had wronged Aboriginal people, his death changed Phillip's kindly approach towards them and he demanded vengeance. His standing orders were that if the troops could not capture the Aborigines responsible then they were to kill *any* six. Despite their best efforts, Phillip's henchmen caught none. And in spite of his more aggressive attitude, Phillip did his best to encourage Aborigines to live within the boundaries of the Port Jackson settlement, where he helped induce them to surrender their freedom and land with the first of 200 odd years' worth of handouts in the form of rations of food and tobacco. It was almost as good a deal as that of the Americans who purchased Manhattan Island from the Indians for a few lousy dollars.

Not all of the Aborigines fell for the white man's ways, however. One, the above-mentioned Pemulwuy, led a bitter resistance from 1790 until he was killed in an ambush by two settlers on the George's River in Sydney's south-west in 1802. During his twelve-year reign he displayed outstanding courage and skills. And while he was the bane of their lives, he won the begrudging respect of the English. Such was Pemulwuy's hero status among his people they believed he could not be killed or defeated, a reputation he earned after he escaped from the Englishmen's chains after being wounded *seven* times in the Battle of Parramatta. He was a noble warrior, yet rather than honour Pemulwuy's fighting spirit the New South Wales Government hacked off his head and sent it to England as a trophy from a far-flung outpost of the Empire. It is said some settlers harboured such a hatred against Pemulwuy they abducted a female member of his family and raped and tortured her—such was the price of his commitment.

Other killings occurred. In the settlers' quest for more land around the Hawkesbury River, a party of soldiers, the New South Wales Corps, was sent to engage the Dharuk people in combat. This they did—in two bloody battles. They decimated the tribe to such an extent that a writer named David Denholm suggested the people of the Dharuk suffered a similar casualty rate to that sustained by the Australian military in World War II— about one in thirty-four. Denholm also pointed out that the war on the Hawkesbury River was a contest between Great Britain and a nation which was outnumbered and without guns but went down fighting. He added that there is no memorial for those who fought and fell in their own country.

There were other battles—Richmond Hill, Brickfield Hill (the western end of Sydney's now bustling George Street), Battle Mountain, Pinjara. And it's true, no memorial stands for those warriors who died in the defence of their land. Indeed, while the British Empire knew and feared the great Zulu leader Chaka and the Maori Hono Heke, no-one bothered to record the name of the mighty Kalkadoon leader who led the charge of Battle Mountain at Cloncurry, Queensland in 1884. In the lead up to the battle, the Kalkadoon had assembled a large arsenal of spears and boomerangs and hidden them among a maze of tall ant hills. A British force advanced to annihilate them. When the white leader, Urquhart, signalled for his men to follow him in a calvary—they charged up the steep slopes of Battle Mountain—the horses couldn't handle the conditions and the 200 riders were forced to dismount and run. However, before their feet left their stirrups they were bombarded with a shower of spears so accurate they forced the once so-sure attackers to run and hide among the rocks like frightened skinks. With the ability to throw four spears before the white troopers could reload their guns, the Kalkadoon pressed home their advantage. At the height of the battle, a powerful warrior knocked Urquhart cold with a chunk of cement-like clay from an ant hill. A trooper shot the warrior dead when he stood upright to finish off the English leader. His failure to kill

Urquhart proved decisive because just as the Kalkadoon appeared to be on the verge of enjoying their first major victory in the hundred-year war, Urquhart rallied. He confused the warriors by dividing his force and attacking two slopes. With mounting casualties the Kalkadoon leader gave an order for his warriors to form ranks and they charged headlong into a wall of bullets with their heavy spears held in front of them like lances. The line wavered, retreated and then reformed to charge again . . . and again. It wasn't warfare, it was murder. By the time the last bullet was fired an estimated 200 Kalkadoon had died. Their bodies were left on the battlefield for the dingoes and crows to feast upon. As a final insult, their sun-bleached bones remained uncovered on the killing fields for many years afterwards.

With the ignorant, ill-conceived words of William Dampier the seeds of the concept of the ignoble Aboriginal savage were sown on the British psyche and used to try to scuttle the world's oldest culture. And what a culture. As I stood on the Survival Day stage the thought struck me that my culture is like a sponge which has had almost all of the water squeezed out of it but there are still a few drops left. Unlike the New Zealand Maoris who kept their culture through the terms of the Treaty of Waintangi, ours was destroyed. I consider that to be one of the worst crimes against us. I don't know the true pride of the Aborigines, which infuriates me, because before the Aboriginal ways were corrupted by the impositions of the white man we had a real sense of community. The young ones had a deep respect for their elders and in return the elders passed on their secrets and wisdom. The land was sacred. All the brothers and sisters shared what they had so no-one ever went hungry. And, more importantly, every man had his dignity.

My generation is the last that can preserve the remaining

strains of it. We can't let our ways die, and to resuscitate them we have to go back to our roots and stay strong. We owe it to the memory of the great warriors who died in the 100-year war with the settlers to fight on.

A lot of people don't understand how hurt I am by the way my people's history reads. Sometimes, when I am alone and I think of the way my grandparents and ancestors lived—and died—it brings tears to my eyes. It hurts me to think that in 1886–87 an author named E.M. Curr made fun of the way in which innocent Aborigines were butchered. In his book *The Australian Race*, he wrote, 'to an observer of languages, it is interesting to note the new significance of the verb *to disperse:* that when a Black girl of fifteen is shot down she is said to be dispersed.' It also pains me to think my grandparents didn't live long enough to see the things I have achieved. You wouldn't believe how many times I have wished they were here to see it, to see my black pride.

My people were once a truly spiritual people. Like Muslims and Christians they believed in a creator but they also had their Dreamtime, the Dreaming. I guess this can most easily be described as our genesis, but even that isn't an entirely true description of it. Traditional Aboriginal belief is that at the dawn of time the world was a great mass of nothingness lying in wait for the mythical beings called the 'ancestors' to arrive and shape the landscape, creating new life as they went. The Dreamtime can be quite abstract and hard to explain because it goes into another dimension. However, there are still Aborigines who live in the wide, sunlit plains of the Northern Territory, or in the shabby, cluttered alleyways which lead to Eveleigh Street in Redfern, who believe they're still living the Dreaming and that every time they do something it leaves an impression on it. I have to tell you this, brother, I would hate to see what the

Dreaming has looked like since that day 212 years ago when the Union Jack was speared into the shores of what the whites called Botany Bay. But here's a brief snapshot:

- **Aborigines have an infant mortality rate five times higher than the national average.**
- **Aborigines live, on average, twenty years less than other Australians.**
- **Aborigines die from diabetes at five times the national average.**
- **Aborigines have a one in four chance of being undernourished.**
- **Aborigines have an atrocious unemployment rate. Almost 50 per cent of indigenous people aged twenty to twenty-four are unemployed.**
- **Aboriginal juveniles are detained in juvenile centres at twenty times the national rate.**
- **Aboriginal children are placed in institutional care at nineteen times the national rate.**
- **Aboriginal children lack Higher School Certificate qualifications. Only one in three complete Year 12, while three in four other Australians complete Year 12.**
- **Aboriginal children aged five to nine years have a one in eight chance of not attending school.**
- **Aboriginal children aged fifteen and over are disadvantaged in terms of education because almost 50 per cent have no formal qualifications.**
- **Aboriginal households live on an income which is about half the national average.**

- **Aborigines face an unemployment rate four times the national average.**
- **Aborigines have a one in three chance of catching trachoma by age nine.**

And then there are other issues which must be resolved: the stolen generations, the much-discussed apology, native title and mandatory sentencing. At the time of writing this book I'm twenty-five years young. But as my reasoning evolves I can't help but cry out against inhumanity, and to fuel my fire I need not look any further than the Aborigines who were hunted down like animals and murdered.

I'm not alone. In 1998 the head of Aboriginal and Islander Research Action, Les Malezer, told the world's press how Aborigines were shot down like kangaroos and their remains sold for the equivalent of a paltry US$75 to museums and private collectors in Britain, Germany, Italy and Holland. Even now, in this so-called 'enlightened' age, the London Natural History Museum is said to hold over 160 Aboriginal remains—yet the administration won't hand them over despite constant requests by Aboriginal and other outraged Australians. If you don't understand how angry that makes us, imagine how the wider Australian community would feel if they heard the Vietnamese not only had the remains of dead diggers in some dank basement in Hanoi but that they thumbed their noses whenever the government asked for their return for a Christian burial. Wouldn't that burn you? Wouldn't it make you want to do something to express your anger?

The Aboriginal remains are somewhere in London, I don't doubt it, but locating them is not only difficult it is also extremely costly. To track down the skull of the great warrior Yagan, who was cut down by bullets in 1833 after he was accused of murdering two shepherds in Western Australia, took many years and $60,000. His head was sent to London as a macabre curio and it was eventually buried in a Liverpool cemetery. After years of negotiation, however, it's back in Australia. But the cry should continue—bring our brothers home! **BRING OUR BROTHERS HOME!**

Killings, brutality and oppression carried on for many, many years. And as I stood on the stage with Christine Anu and other great Aboriginal achievers I couldn't help but think of the public outrage about numerous boatloads of illegal immigrants from Indonesia and the Middle East landing on Australian soil. It seemed ironic, because the Aborigines who saw Phillip and his human cargo arrive at Botany Bay all those years ago made it clear they weren't welcome. Yet, they stayed. They bred like the rabbits they introduced from Europe, and like the rabbits they ruined the country. However, they also crushed a race's spirit. They made us the bottom of the barrel. And when I think of the cruelty my people have endured—the rape, the pillaging, the murder, the loss of land, the stolen generations—I feel that had I been one of those brave warriors who rattled their spears at Cook and his crew as they approached Kurnell, I would have fought to the death, brother. Nothing surer.

# CHAPTER 8

# THE STOLEN GENERATIONS

*I don't live my life for me anymore. I live for her...*
**My public proclamation for Jada, the Sun Herald, 26 September 1999**

I have many passions in my life, but when it comes to love, few things match my feelings for my baby girl, Jada. At the time of my writing this book, Jada is only nineteen months old, but, take it from me, I've grown into a man during that year and a half. She has not only given me tremendous joy but has provided me with another real reason to do something great with my life. Before I go any further, I have taken time out to pen a letter to Jada, and I hope that when she's old enough to read it she'll realise how much her daddy loves her. I'd die for her.

7 March 2000, 9.35 p.m.
The Spy Cafe
Pitt Street, Sydney

To My Darling Daughter,

Well, baby, you're nineteen months now and you're not with me at the moment. It's 9.30 at night and you're probably asleep at Mummy's. As I write this message to you it's my hope that one day in the years to come when you're able to read, you'll receive my message loud and clear.

Jada, every time you enter my mind you make me want to

smile. Knowing I'll be seeing you soon puts that extra bounce in my step, honey. All I wish is for you to know whatever you want to achieve in your life you have your Daddy's support, and I'll be there for you in the good and the bad times no matter what.

Sometimes, baby, I lay in my bed and I shed me a tear . . . but it's of joy, sweetheart. I just want to be equal to the task of helping to bring you up right, in the best possible way. I want to be there to guide you.

I'll say bye now but you know goodbyes are never forever because I'll be in your heart for as long as you live.

I love you, Daddy's Girl.

In the Muslim religion we have a saying about a baby being a blessing from God—and it could have been penned especially for little Jada. She has opened my eyes to a side of life I didn't expect to experience for a few years down the track—fatherhood. This is a time for selflessness and love. Everything I do, I do it for her. She always brightens my day. I think of her smile and I laugh. If I'm in a bad mood I think of her and the dark clouds disappear. Even if I don't achieve anything else in my life I think being able to boast I'm her father isn't a bad thing to hang my hat on.

Jada's mother is Danielle. She's of African–American descent and she's a generous woman and brilliant mother.

It's when I think of my love for Jada that I get an insight into the pain of the parents and kids of the stolen generations. Before I played in the 1999 Grand Final against Melbourne I dedicated my appearance in that game to the stolen generations of Aborigines—but none more so than to my Grandma Audrey. How hard that part of her life must have been. Some people thought my declaration was too political for their liking but I didn't care. I hoped to let those who'd had their lives affected by the criminal ways of the old governments know that some-one cared for them. Australia has done many, many terrible things to its indigenous people and I've already cited some of them. But the idea of the government and church taking babies and kids from their families—*in the child's best interest*—makes my hot blood run cold. The feeling of utter devastation felt by both parties must have been a pain too much for them to bear, a pain from which they could never hope to recover. If some-one from a government department had tried to take Jada from me I would have freaked. Knowing my love for her, I don't know what I would have done. Thinking of parents trying to paint their children's skin a darker shade so the authorities wouldn't want them makes me furious.

The policy of removing some Aboriginal children from their parents, which stopped in 1970, was designed to break down the Aboriginal culture. Indigenous kids with an ounce of Caucasian blood were taken from their families to be assimilated into white Australia. Some were sent out to white families, others were sent to properties, still others were left to the mercy of the churches—and in those stakes the churches were close to bankrupt.

It was drummed into the children's heads that they were white. I've read, and heard, of how nuns constantly hammered it into their young minds that they weren't black—regardless of their skin colour. Some were even encouraged to explain their complexion by saying they came from southern Europe. This train of thought wasn't restricted to the churches, because evi-dence suggests some foster parents told their kids that black people were bad. One woman was brought up to believe her mother was a promiscuous drunk, but when she finally met her mum the girl started crying. The mother asked why her baby was shedding tears and when she embraced her, the daughter felt a surge of love and warmth only a mother can provide. The next time this woman saw her mother, she was in an open casket.

And the authorities did what they could to discourage the stolen generations from hanging onto their culture. Missionaries told the children their own language was the devil's language and washed their mouths out with soap. This made them forget their own language. I've heard of a woman whose bloodlines were only acknowledged when she was in trouble and being punished, and they'd call her 'Abo' or 'nigger'.

Many members of the stolen generations have complained about being underfed in the camps they were sent to—some were even given straw in their diet. Others were confused by the lessons of the Christians who'd teach them about love, and then bash them.

There were various means of humiliation. The former West Australian Chief Protector A.O. Neville described some of the punishments dealt out at one settlement, including the case of a superintendent who tarred and feathered an Aborigine. When he finished he called the staff to see the 'rare bird' he'd captured. Another superintendent chained a girl's legs to table legs; another shaved girls' heads bald and dressed them in old sacks in an effort to degrade them.

The law of the jungle existed in many of the camps the kids were sent to. In one, if the children answered back to an attendant they were 'sent up the line' which meant their brothers, cousins and friends punched them. If any refused to lash out they were forced to run up the line themselves, and more often than not several kids finished up with broken noses and busted ribs. In the 1930s and 1940s the cat-o'-nine-tails, the same weapon used on the early convicts, was used to punish the children.

As an Aborigine who grew up in a loving family, what

*really* hurts me is thinking that while these kids were being brutalised and shamed their parents were at home pining for them. And this is before I take into account the other nightmares like sexual abuse. I understand the Kinchela camp was hell on earth. Boys had sex with each other and a manager was actually imprisoned for sexual abuse. He wasn't alone though, because an English bloke had also taken advantage of the defenceless kids. Many children were allegedly sexually abused in institutions. One man sent to an orphanage in the 1930s claimed there was 'tampering' with the boys. He said the people who worked with the kids would fondle the boys' penises and play around with them. It was an absolute betrayal of trust. A woman removed to a girls' home in the 1940s was subjected to constant 'ignorant' rape when she was just nine or ten. It was 'ignorant rape' because she would munch on the puffed wheat that had been used to lure her into the room while the woman superintendent inserted a piece of wood in and out of her vagina.

A woman who was removed in the 1960s complained to the police about her foster father tampering with her, but they thought she was lying. The foster mother also called her a liar and she was placed in a hostel for wild children. Because of her treatment when she dared to speak out, this lady bottled her pain and anger up and said nothing about it again for years. Another woman who was removed from her family in the 1940s when she was only three spoke of the constant fear she lived with. She was afraid to undress to have a bath and was scared of the dark because her foster father molested her. She once tried to tell the local priest and he told her to say ten Hail Marys for telling lies.

Some children were luckier; they found love and affection in their foster homes. That was the exception rather than the rule, however, and the individuals who found such a home knew to be grateful.

So what does all this mean? Well, listen up and I'll tell you.

- **The majority of the 300,000 Aborigines living in Australia come from families directly affected by the removal of some children.**
- **Many of the children never saw their parents again.**
- **Some Aborigines are worried they might be unwittingly marrying or dating their sister or brother because they have no idea who their relatives are.**
- **Many Aborigines imprisoned around the nation are members of the stolen generations.**
- **Forty-three out of the 100 Aborigines who died in custody during the 1980s were victims of government removal policies.**
- **The child removal policies violated provisions of the 1948 Universal Declaration of Human Rights and other international treaties.**
- **Aboriginal children faced punishment if they spoke their native language or escaped to return home.**

All the Aborigines from the stolen generations have asked for is an official apology from Prime Minister John Howard. But while he's expressed his sorrow he refuses, as leader of the nation, to apologise for the sins of his fathers. The government doesn't believe the victims should have any right to stake a financial claim for compensation. While the government is drawing up treaties with foreign lands to extradite alleged Nazi war criminals for crimes committed against the Jews in World War II, they've made no commitment to investigate the claims made by their own citizens, albeit black ones, about sexual and physical abuse.

Indeed, while Australia stumbles and fumbles, the Municipality of Florence, Italy, approved a motion in 1999 concerning those Aboriginal people who were affected by Australian government policies. The motion, proposed by the Italian branch of the German-based Society for Threatened Peoples, has called upon the Howard government to pay compensation to affected families. The motion was seen as the first step in a European campaign which will try to involve the Italian Senate as well as the European Parliament. If that pressure is applied to Australia—a country which won universal praise for intervening in East Timor—it will be an embarrassment as it places the spotlight on the nation's human rights record.

As I was writing this book it distressed me no end to read a report in the *Australian* newspaper that research commissioned by the Council for Aboriginal Reconciliation showed most Aussies are strongly against apologising to Aborigines. The article said the 170-page report would be used by Howard to justify his decision to abandon his heartfelt election night promise for reconciliation before the centenary of Federation on 1 January 2001. The study is said to have found ignorance rather than racism. It seemed the four things which worried most white Australians were land rights, compensation for past wrongs, welfare handouts and the act of apologising.

Listen up, I'm not happy with John Howard. I look forward to the next time we cross paths because I'm going to set him straight on this issue. His advisors are obviously giving him the wrong information because these wounds—these many bloody wounds—won't ever heal unless he does something positive. If you want to get an idea of how I feel about him and his spine-lessness on this matter consider my reaction when I was introduced to him at the Grand Final. I didn't look at him and the hand I offered when he stuck his out was a 'wet fish'. I should have ignored him completely, as he has ignored the continued suffering of my people. It's not a personal thing—if Kim Beazley were in power and treated the issue the same way then I'd react accordingly. Prime Minister Howard might be right in thinking an apology won't heal all wounds but it would at least be some sort of a start. In fact, it might just help some Aborigines understand that the degradations they endured as innocent children were no fault of their own.

Howard, hear the cries of your black people!

# CHAPTER 9

# THE BLOCK

During the early stages of the 2000 season I had a brain-wave I would take a few of my old St George-Illawarra team-mates down to 'The Block', Eveleigh Street, to see the place for themselves. While they'd heard plenty of stories concerning riots, bashings, robberies, police raids and drugs, they had no idea of what really to expect.

We had no preconceived plans to go there; it was just a night out cruising about town. But after taking a few turns left, and then a right from Parramatta Road, we ended up driving down *the* street itself, and I pulled up so the boys could take in the sights and the sounds of the place—the urban battle zone—they'd heard so much about courtesy of frantic media reports and folklore. The boys saw The Block in all its tragic glory: derelict houses, rubble, empty beer cans, used syringes strewn over the place, shattered windows, drunken men lounging about and kids with snotty noses playing footy. But they also met my cousins and friends, proud people who take pride not only in being Aboriginal but also in their grand dreams of rising above their lot and making a stand. But that's Eveleigh Street, brother. It's a place with no absolute truths, just grey zones and shadows.

In ancient times Redfern was the domain of the Gadigal people, but for modern day Aborigines it's probably the safest place—safer even than the trendy Eastern Suburbs—because, despite the media's preoccupation with bad reports about the place, my people aren't in the minority there. It's a place where Aborigines are related by both blood *and* community. They each share the same hopes and fears as well as the same social and economic conditions. Indeed, Eveleigh Street and the surrounding areas are seen by many Aborigines as sacred ground—and there is justification for such sentiment. You see, my people have been drawn to the Redfern area since the 1930s, the days when the factories and railways offered unskilled labourers the opportunity to make an honest living. (The factories and jobs have long gone, and that has played a role in the breakdown in Redfern society.) When Aborigines arrived in the big smoke from the country in search of work Redfern was usually their first port of call. But despite black people's presence in the area they not only experienced racially motivated harassment from the police, but very few were allowed to obtain permanent housing in the district.

Regardless of this unwelcome attention from the law, Redfern became home to the Aboriginal Progressive Association, the group which was instrumental in organising the Day of Mourning in 1938. When white Australia celebrated the sesquicentenary of European settlement, Aborigines from all around the nation congregated in Redfern before marching on Australia Hall in Elizabeth Street to demand their human rights.

In November 1972, Redfern again became the focal point of Aboriginal hope when sixteen young Aborigines were arrested for squatting in terrace houses along Louis Street. Rather than add yet another chapter to the Aborigines' book of lament and wrongdoing, their appearance in court sowed seeds of hope for the Aborigines of Redfern. This was because a young black lawyer named Peter Hidden managed to obtain bail—a feat which was unheard of in those days—and the men were released into the custody of Father Ted Kennedy of St Vincent's Church, Redfern.

By the end of the week 100 Aborigines had crammed into the church hall, highlighting how desperate their accommodation crisis was. The South Sydney Council responded by serving an eviction notice on the Archdiocese of Sydney. But rather than take things lying down, a group of the young men returned to Louis Street to claim the abandoned homes as their own. As a sign of solidarity the Builders and Labourers Federation provided help and the houses were soon outfitted with plumbing and electricity. While the squatters arranged to buy the houses from Mr Ian Kiernan—who now heads Clean Up Australia—they were subjected to constant police harassment. Yet, the men and women refused to yield, and despite a history of defeats and grim losses to the whites Redfern was one battle the Aborigines won. In its wisdom the Whitlam government released the funds—half a million dollars—needed to buy Kiernan's twenty-five properties, and by doing so the Aborigines ended up owning the block of real estate bounded by Caroline, Vine, Eveleigh and Louis Streets. It became our own piece of turf in Sydney. The tenants were black and so too were the landlords and for the first time since Arthur Phillip headed the First Fleet to Port Jackson, Aboriginal customs and sensitivities shaped everyday life in part of central Sydney.

In those hopeful early days there were plans for it to become a black utopia, with talk of smashing down all the fences so the backyards could form a common green for the children to play. It didn't eventuate. Those early 'pioneers' spoke of The Block being a kingdom where Aborigines would walk around like kings and queens—the former Australian boxing champion Dick Blair said it would be silly to say it would become a ghetto—but it tragically all went wrong. The old Koori demon, alcohol—and then drugs—eroded what was a great community. It wasn't just the grog, though. The place fell into a state of disrepair because the rents being charged for the properties—$55 per week for a two-bedroom house and $60 for a three-bedroom one—were too cheap to maintain the buildings. With the breakdown came the need to take drastic action, and almost thirty years after the Aborigines reclaimed Eveleigh Street, some tenants were being relocated and houses were being demolished. It was a tragedy, and as one long-term Block local, Mrs Buchanan, told the press, 'The dream has soured like milk in the sun.'

Over the years, this cluttered street has been described as many things, including a 'no-go zone', 'Sydney's Harlem', 'Australia's version of Soweto, South Africa' and a 'racial hot spot'. Nevertheless, I'm sure what my team-mates witnessed that night opened their eyes to the plight of the blackfella; I know it moved Matt Cooper, Chris Leikvoll, Luke Bailey, Jason Hooper and Luke Patten when they saw for themselves the hopelessness of Eveleigh Street. That was important to me because over the years a few of the guys have tried to bait me at training about my outspoken views on Aboriginal issues by talking about 'government handouts' and the perceived 'laziness' of the brothers. Indeed, some of them said I should be happy to have benefited from the 'white man's' presence and system because I made good money from football.

While it hurt me to hear that kind of talk I never thought ill of the blokes and their views. I realise they don't understand the helplessness and the anguish of the Aborigines. I'm sure if they did they'd hold their tongues and rise above the rubbish indoctrinated in them via the media and government authorities over the years. They'd come to realise that we Aborigines think differently from white people, best summed up by Cathy Craigie in the *Sydney Morning Herald* a few years ago:

My idea of white Australia is about having the house and the little picket fence. For Aboriginal Australia these things don't matter. Our association is with the land, not where you buy a house. People think because we dress the same and use the same language, our aspirations are the same. They're not.

I'm often asked about my own views on the Aboriginal way of sharing what we have, and, yes, I do help brothers out. I'm not silly. I know who really needs help and who is looking for a handout. But my view is if you can help a brother out of trouble then you do everything possible. However, rather than throw the cash around willy-nilly, I have set aside a proportion of money which is used to help worthwhile Aboriginal and individual causes.

While I was growing up in Earlwood, a middle class suburb in south-west Sydney, I was exposed to the ways of Eveleigh Street through going to my father's gymnasium, which is still based slap-bang in the middle of the place. My uncle Mick runs the housing co-op at the top of the street. So I've seen the struggle from close proximity and I've also borne witness to the place degenerating from a once harmonious community into a fractured society ruined by an influx of hard drugs and alcohol. And what hurts me, *what really burns me*, is that a lot of the young people I see walking around looking for a 'hit' or a swig of grog were once bright-eyed kids who had talent, hopes and dreams. However, belonging to an underclass has turned them into nothing more than zonked-out zombies, and I cry for them.

I'm certain the white politicians are happy to let them behave in that manner because it helps to manifest—and perpetuate—the belief that my people are nothing more than petrol-sniffing, drug-taking, dirty beggars who'll sell their soul for cheap grog. But that's crap, man. It isn't our way. For 40,000 years we were anything but that. We had no idea of alcohol until the arrival of the British and even then we didn't immediately embrace it. The demon drink was pushed upon us. Yet, over the centuries the white system of stripping the Aborigines of their rights and dignity has made them dependent upon first the drink, and now upon drugs. It's not so much the average white Australian who has caused the problem; it's the people of power who have realised substance dependence is the next best thing to the old style massacres. Believe me, what the government is allowing to happen to the Aborigines in Eveleigh Street—and other reservations—is just as bad as the early days of colonisation when they handed out blankets infected with smallpox.

It's a conspiracy. Eveleigh Street is watched by surveillance cameras—they've been there for years—and the police can see the kids shooting up and they can see the deals that are being made. If they *really* wanted to stop it they could, but the reason they choose not to get involved is because it's so easy to keep people under control when they're dependent upon both addictive substances and social welfare handouts. As I have already said, drugs and grog just aren't the way of the Aborigine: in 200 years—a twinkling in time's eye—it's been brought undone.

The media pushes the line that Aborigines want to live the way they do in Eveleigh Street and other reservations, but I tell you it's not true. If you saw Eveleigh Street, Palm Island, or any of the other reservations, you'd dismiss them as living hells. Do you really think we want to live like that? I'm certain if you took an eight year old there and said, 'Boy, this is where you're going to live, amid the used syringes, the broken beer bottles, the rats and the disease called Aboriginal hopelessness' he'd bawl man, he'd bawl like a little baby. The places where they've hidden my people are all the same. The people based there aren't living, they're just hanging on by their fingertips—and that certainly wasn't a part of our lifestyle before the white man arrived.

I often hear people talk about the Aboriginal race being born lazy, but that's not true. Living as fringe dwellers stems from a lifetime of constant rejection at school and then at the workplace. If you think I'm making up excuses, here's a scenario for you to consider: if an Aboriginal boy were to apply for a job with you and there was a kid of the same age and a different nationality after the same position, who would *you* employ? Now ask yourself how many 'no's' can an Aborigine— or anyone for that matter—take? And it's with each setback that the vicious cycle of poverty forms. The Aborigine can't get a job; they have no chance of getting money; the younger Aborigines see their brothers' plight and wonder why should they worry about schooling and education because they aren't going to get anywhere. So the Aborigine turns to crime for cash; seeks ways to escape and turns to drink and drugs because they make them feel good, at least for a little while; turns their back on responsibility; their health deteriorates. Soon they are seen as a layabout; they get in trouble with the law and go to court; the judge sentences them to a stint in prison. On the inside they learn to hate anything which represents white authority and their family falls apart; when they return to the outside they lose their last hope in a drunken blur and one morning die of heart failure, or some other illness, before their time. And, as is the way with the circle of life, along the way another young Aborigine has been born to inherit their misery.

The time has arrived for the Australian government—the Australian people—to ask themselves what a black life is really worth? How can they stand by and watch this state of hopelessness? Aren't they ashamed to think the United Nations is investigating the treatment of the black people here?

As I have said, it isn't just Eveleigh Street. And it's true; we have no great culture anymore, it's dying a fast death. In the Northern Territory remnants of it have survived, but that's all. The reservations themselves are nothing for Australians to be proud of. Those communities are more often than not in the middle of nowhere. The hygiene and health standards are unacceptable and, if you read the views of Justice Marcus Einfield on the conditions at Toomelah in New South Wales, they're the next best thing to a concentration camp. 'There may not be high fences or SS guards around Toomelah,' Einfield told the *Age* in 1987, 'but if you live in a house with 21 others, cannot get out of town because the road is impassable, or cannot get to work, you live in a prison . . . it is well that Australians, all of us, should see that Toomelah exists because of us and what we are as Australians.'

To return to The Block though, the mainstream media has long made an issue of the hostility between the police and the residents of Eveleigh Street. Yet, what do the police expect when they instigate raids in the dead of night, and upturn beds, break furniture, kick people and their families out on the street? And what are they looking for? It's when the man of the house is standing shivering on the street and looking at his defenceless family that he begins to feel as if he is seen as nothing more than a savage. And that's when the anger and the hatred explodes inside of him and he lashes out. He's reached the zone of no return. Then, when the next police car patrols the street an hour or two afterwards, cops are set upon. What kind of reception do they expect? A welcome?

That anger and frustration is something the Aborigines in The Block have to get out of their system. Otherwise they'll go mad. In February 1990, the police instigated a raid in the dead of night, moving in with sledgehammers and search warrants. Not long after, a young Eveleigh Street resident told of the feelings the police tactics cause: 'The police push their way in here. They come with reinforcements. And what do you expect us blackfellas to do? We have to show 'em we have guts. We will charge back and when we charge back that is when things explode.'

In 1992, a coloured South African photographer named Peter McKenzie described Eveleigh Street as being very similar to District Six, a very poor black area of Cape Town—although he added that the Australian Aborigine and the black South African were different because we have the right to vote. 'The difference between Australia and South Africa,' McKenzie observed, 'is that apartheid is not legislation here . . . but there is a kind of social apartheid at work in suburbs such as Redfern.'

While the political climate has changed in South Africa since then, the champion jockey Darren Beadman became familiar with that sense of apartheid McKenzie spoke of when he would make his way down Eveleigh Street in his capacity as a religious minister, handing out loaves of fresh bread and donuts to the people of The Block. Before his return to racing, Darren's turf was a far cry from the glamour and wealth of Australia's lucrative horseracing circuit—but I'm sure the experience helped him grow spiritually. Indeed, there was once a time when Beadman would press down hard on the accelerator of his flashy sports car to race past the place.

He told a reporter:

This is a tough place, a hard place. I would drive past Eveleigh Street on my way to some race meetings and I would think there was no way I would ever go down there. It's funny how life changes. I was always aware there was poverty. However, I was always riding and I didn't have much to do with it. But when I'm asked whether giving away bread helps, then I think, yes . . . yes it does because every bit helps when you have nothing. Actually, it's a blessing.

Nevertheless, Beadman also saw the uglier side of Eveleigh Street and it sickened him. While he could see plenty of good in the young Aboriginal kids who would run to 'high five' him, he was well aware that many of the kids—like little Gary who at age seven joined his uncle in regularly cleaning the street of used syringes—are much older than their years suggest.

> Look at them, they're innocent and pure and we have to pro-tect that sense of innocence. I've found the problem with the society they grow up in is it hardens their head and spirit and it's hard to bring them back from that. It sometimes feels as if they are caught in a spider's web and it takes a lot to break them free of it. They live hard. Look at that, you have little kids picking up used syringes off the ground. What does that do to them? We came across a kid in an alley and he had a tourni-quet wrapped around his arm and he was heating up a spoon. He was only three . . . three years old. Yeah, they grow up quick here but it is up to people like me to teach them to keep clear of drugs. Drugs kill, they destroy families and they make the user steal and cheat . . . it's evil.

As I've said, it's not just Eveleigh Street. At Palm Island, in trop-ical North Queensland, the locals also yearn for the old days when there was a sense of community. Their lives too have been eroded by drugs, drink and youth suicide. One Palm Islander, Leuella Bligh, told the press of the changes she has noticed on the island. She said there had always been plenty to do, for example, old-time dancing and sports. The emphasis was on family and everyone had a vegie garden and a chook run. She said that now there's nothing for kids to do and that drugs and alcohol were ruining the island.

Another local pointed out to the same reporter that the lack of hope and opportunity on Palm Island was now so strong that if there was a little girl there who had the potential to be another Cathy Freeman, she wouldn't get anywhere unless she left.

Unfortunately, there has been a breakdown in the younger generation's approach to their elders. It's not just Aborigines who are guilty of this—it's a universal thing, and the world is paying a sad price for it.

Nonetheless one of the great problems in Eveleigh Street is the fact that the elders have lost their hold over the younger generation. Before, a troublemaker would be disciplined according to law, the tribal law handed down by the elders, and it included anything from being banished from the area to a thrashing. Some might shake their heads in disgust, but it worked because no Aborigine dared to do wrong by another brother, be it stealing or assault. In 1997, a reporter from the *Australian* named Elisabeth Wynhausen observed a kid playing truant. His mother had died of an overdose and his father had hanged himself. She first saw him with another boy on the roof of a derelict building, hurling condom water bombs at a woman picking up syringes left lying around Caroline Lane. The woman screamed a few warnings and heaved a half brick up towards them.

The epitaph for Eveleigh Street is perhaps best summed up by Joyce Ingram. In June 1990, the resident said of the place white Australia describes as a 'pockmarked' street, that she'd been there all her life and that there was nothing wrong with Eveleigh Street except for a lot of bad publicity. She said that a lot of the kids were dropouts and out of stride with the older people. 'We have so many tribes here. They are not great big groups—four or five people—but there is a division among them and when problems start they band together. But it's not as bad here as people say.'

As for poverty being called the 'black man's disease', I fear there'll always be poor people but they don't have to live on the brink. In a nation such as Australia no person should go to bed wishing they had something extra that night to fill their belly. But poverty is a vicious cycle for the downtrodden because few job opportunities means low incomes, which result in no savings, which equates with no hope. In such an environment some parents lose control over their kids and they run wild, get in trouble with the law and start life behind the eight ball. We have to create jobs; we have to find another Snowy Mountains scheme to employ the masses. It comes back to hope, home, education.

The fact is, however, that the Aborigine is a poor person in an affluent society—and they know they're being screwed. They see other people with flashy cars, good clothes and jewellery and they wonder why others have so much and a kind of resentment grows. It happens all over the world where you have an underclass. A lot of kids try their best to stay on the straight and narrow but others will be driven to take the short cut and find other ways of obtaining what they want.

A recent survey taken by the Australian Bureau of Statistics of Aboriginal and Torres Strait Islander households provided this snapshot of Aboriginal households:

- **59 per cent of Aborigines aged fifteen years and over had an annual income of less than $12,000**
- **11 per cent had an annual income over $25,000**
- **the government provided 55 per cent with their main source of income**

- **11 per cent had no income**
- **according to the survey, the mean annual income for Aborigines was $14,406–$15,448 for men and $12,702 for women.**

An estimated 116,400 received government incomes:

- **43 per cent received family support**
- **32 per cent received Jobstart or Jobsearch allowances**
- **16 per cent were on single parent payments, 92 per cent of them being women.**

So you can see there isn't much room for self-indulgence if you're Aboriginal. The average Aussie has to realise greed is bad. We have to step back and realise people are more than consumers; they're human beings. They're flesh and blood and each individual has individual needs.

The well-documented Aboriginal health problems start when the babies are born with a low birth weight, and then, as they grow older, Aborigines fare much worse than other Australians. In 1996, for instance, 80 per cent of the children affected by pneumonia were of Aboriginal descent. Four times as many Aborigines have diabetics as non-indigenous Aussies. Malnutrition too is a problem, so when you look at the overall situation it comes as no surprise that life expectancy among my people is very short. We need more medical facilities, we need to establish a major education program on good health and nutrition—and we need to get Aborigines into the medical profession. Obviously budgets are a concern, but people are our greatest resource and we have to get out among the community and find out what the common problems are and then work on solving them. It's simply not good enough to let people have a substandard existence. If that means we have to pay doctors extra to live in the outback and that we have to build satellite hospitals in the outer suburbs, then we'll just have to do it. Maybe, just maybe, we can start by selling some of the many paintings hanging in the hallways and offices of Parliament House in Canberra . . .

# CHAPTER 10

# COPPING COPS

*With some noble exceptions, we failed to make the most basic human response and enter into their hearts and minds. We failed to ask—how would I feel if this were done to me? As a consequence, we failed to see that what we were doing degraded all of us.*

*If we needed a reminder of this, we received it this year. The Report of the Royal Commission into Aboriginal Deaths in Custody showed with devastating clarity that the past lives on in inequity, racism and injustice in the prejudice and ignorance of non-Aboriginal Australians, and in the demoralisation and desperation, the fractured identity, of so many Aborigines and Torres Strait Islanders.*

*Prime Minister Paul Keating's speech for the Year of the World's Indigenous People, 1992*

One thing you learn quickly when you're an Aboriginal kid is that there's no such thing as minding your own business. I lost count a long time ago of the number of times the cops hassled my 'brothers' and me whenever we were drawn into Sydney by the bright lights and the prospect of a good night out. We weren't thieves, we weren't public enemies, we weren't there to make trouble, because we were too scared to step out of line for fear of what our parents would do to us if we got into *any* strife! Yet, the cops didn't care about that.

They'd shake us down in front of the passing parade on George Street, Sydney's main movie and video arcade drag. There's a routine—and I reckon every Aboriginal kid knows it back to front. The sergeant asks for your name, he demands to know what you're doing in the city, he scribbles down your address and phone number, then he warns you'll go straight to the boys' home if you muck up! If he's an older copper he might add how much he regrets it's now against the law for him to give you a kick up the arse, and send you home. So, as we'd stand looking shamefaced and annoyed, people headed for the movies and restaurants would look down at us as if we were common criminals. While drunken businessmen would stumble past, wide-eyed mothers and fathers from middle class suburbia would stare at us as if we were playing out a scene from the television show *N.Y.P.D.* They probably figured we'd been busted for selling—or buying—drugs, hassling the pretty white girls we'd sometimes talk to outside McDonalds or, even worse, they might have thought we'd been pulled up for stealing an old woman's handbag. But, I swear, we were just kids out on the town for some innocent fun. Our only crime was our complexion—and we were repeat offenders in that regard because our grandfathers were black, our dads are black and we're black.

I speak from experience when I say if you're black in Australia and in an area where things are going on, the general assumption is you're up to no good. Believe me, from my side of the fence—the dark half—the law of the land is based upon foundations of assumption and prejudice. That means if you're black, you're guilty! If you belong to a minority group with no political punch—and that's the Aborigines—then you're right behind the eight ball. You're open game and you have no chance. You go to a place like George Street and the cops take down your name and *every* time you return they watch you like a hawk, watching and waiting for you to *look* as if you're about to do something so they can ice you. You might ask why we return knowing full well that we're going to be pulled up and shaken down. Why shouldn't we? Why should we be fringe dwellers when Australia is supposed to be a free country? All the police achieved with their notepads and wisecracks about us being 'Abos from Eveleigh Street' was to upset us, ruin our night out and foster a deep hatred towards them in our hearts.

You go to school and the teachers say to respect the law. Then you go out like thousands of so-called 'normal' kids and you realise the law doesn't respect you. It judges me and my friends by the colour of our skin, not our worth as individuals. The smart kids—and I was one—quickly learn not to talk back, to give short answers and to show no impatience. Being confronted by a police officer—and I'm sure it's the same all over the nation—is akin to coming face to face with a shark in the ocean. Under no circumstance do you show any fear because they can smell it and that is their signal to maul you, physically or verbally.

Unfortunately, going to prison or getting in trouble with the police has almost become a part of life for most Aboriginal teenage boys—indeed, it's almost replaced some of the old tribal initiations. In Australia's two largest states, in terms of land area, Western Australia and Queensland, half the number of children in prison or boys' homes are indigenous, even though they make up less than 5 per cent of the Australian population under the age of eighteen. In 1997, statistics from the Australian Institute of Criminology showed nearly 50 per cent of Aborigines aged between eighteen to twenty-four have been arrested by police on at least one occasion. The way in which some of them are treated is deplorable and should instigate demonstrations outside the United Nations. For instance, there was the time a fifteen year old was ordered by a magistrate to spend a month in custody—in a prison 600 kilometres from his home—for pinching an ice-cream worth $1.90. The Children's Court of Western Australia intervened and had him released after ruling the sentence inappropriate.

As I grew older I found the police attention intensified. I can well remember the terrible fear I felt one evening when my cousin Wes Patten parked his car alongside mine—both were full of Aborigines—in a backstreet in Waterloo. While we tried to work out our next move—to cruise downtown or drop in on some friends to watch videos—two police patrol cars screamed around the corner, sirens wailing. When they screeched to a halt they'd blocked us in. For the life of me I had no idea what was happening—and by the look on Wes's face, nor did he. The policemen jumped out of their cars with their guns drawn. Above the din of the sirens and the thumping of my heart I heard them scream for us to get out of our vehicles with our hands on our heads. I looked into their eyes and they were pumped. The boys in blue meant business. One had spit in the corner of his mouth, another's face was twisted with rage and another had his finger so tightly gripped on the trigger of his pistol I figured he'd already decided there'd be some black blood spilt before the encounter was over. I focused on him and waited. I waited for the finger to move and to hear the terrible bang that spells death. Thankfully, it didn't come, and as the seconds ticked by I waited and wondered. I didn't want to die, man, I was only twenty and a series of fears ran through my mind. Would I die? Would they leave Wes, me and the others face down and bleeding in the gutter in a filthy alleyway I didn't even know the name of? Would they tell the investigators we went for a gun? Would they get in trouble?

My heart sounded like the pulse of a rap song. I didn't dare to turn my head to look at Wes because I didn't want to spook the lawmen. No sudden movements, man, it's the law of survival. You don't do anything to set them over the edge when they have their guns trained on your head.

I don't know how long the standoff lasted. It could have

been thirty seconds or three minutes; time really does stand still in such a circumstance. And then, suddenly, the police put their guns away and one of them snapped. He screamed at us and I couldn't understand what he was on about. But his aggression triggered something deep within Wes, because my little cousin started barking back. After years of harassment they had got to him and he lost it. A lot of what he had to say was lost in his screams of rage, but his anger was unmistakable. And it's true, it does get to you.

You see, Wes was also the centre of a police-related racial slur when he was called a 'coon' by a copper during the filming of a documentary for the ABC a few years ago. He took the officer concerned to court and it was found the cop had breached the anti-discrimination laws.

However, we didn't even lodge a complaint about this Waterloo incident. We knew the cops would just make excuses; they'd say we were acting suspiciously or that we'd done something to provoke them. We let it go, but the anger, the shame and the hurt never leaves you because, I have to say, I never felt as helpless as I did when that gun was aimed square at my face. You don't ever forget those kind of experiences, because they cut deep. Even so, you have to try to overcome them, otherwise you'll stay clinging to the bottom rung.

While I was definitely harassed by police as a kid, I fared a lot better than some others. In Western Australia, for instance, there's a case of a young boy who was hounded to death by the cops, and his, I'm afraid, is not an isolated case. Aboriginal history is crammed with similar stories, but they're mostly dismissed with a wave of white contempt. Western Australia is regarded as the 'sorrow state' for modern day Aborigines because more of our brothers and sisters are imprisoned there than in any other part of Australia. The boy I speak of first came to the attention of police when he was alleged to have been choking two other boys. He was led away from the playground by two officers and, to teach the lad a harsh lesson, they locked him in a cell. After his brush with the law the boy's life went into a downward spiral. He was constantly suspended for fighting other students and abusing school staff and a report on his troubled, young years tells a shameful story.

- **5 March 1997: Four cops arrive at his house because he allegedly broke a window. Despite him being just eleven years old a cop is said to have assaulted him with a baton before dragging him away to the station.**
- **28 April 1997: The boy is taken into custody after a policeman saw him with a lamp and other property. The officer concerned believed a report had been filed about the lamp— investigations revealed there had been none.**
- **5 May 1997: The boy is seen doubling a friend on a pushbike. He wasn't wearing a helmet, but the police took him away for questioning because they thought the bike had been reported stolen. No such report had been made.**
- **9 May 1997: The kid is taken back to the station for yet another chat with his pals in blue because he was wearing a cheap necklace. The cops seized the necklace from him.**
- **23 May 1997: An officer apprehends the boy during a street parade because he abused an elderly man he bumped into. The officer believed there was a bench warrant for his**

**arrest. He is charged for burglary of a vacant house and released on bail with a 7 p.m. curfew condition.**

- **3 June 1997: The boy and his cousin are play-fighting in the front garden of a house. When they run off and jump a fence they're charged with two offences of being on premises without a lawful excuse.**
- **6 June 1997: The boy's mother picks him up from a roller-skating disco because he's in breach of his curfew. Later that night he hangs himself—commits suicide—at just eleven years of age.**

It's disgraceful. It is a sickening, poison tale. How can any kid be so bad that the police chase him to his grave? Oh, wake up Australia. WAKE UP . . . WAKE UP. You're sleeping through injustices of the worst kind.

The coronial inquest recorded an open verdict on the basis the boy was probably too young to appreciate his actions. The local cops described it as a tragedy. The *West Australian* epitaph was that the kid's death offered a final ray of hope that police would lay off using batons when apprehending children.

But this is not an isolated case. The list goes on and on.

And what of the fate of the Aboriginal prisoners on the inside? They, more often than not, endure a living hell. The West Australian Deaths in Custody Watch Committee addressed the use of isolation cells at Casuarina, which is straight out of the Middle Ages. Six wardens extract a prisoner from his cell by binding and gagging him, then applying a body belt and shackles. The prisoner is pulled to his feet and forced to run to the punishment area where his clothes are cut off, and he's left naked and shackled in the cell. He has no access to daylight, visitors or telephone calls during his time in solitary confinement and can be there for months on end. Every meal is eaten on the floor because furniture isn't permitted in the cell.

And then there are the mandatory sentencing laws of Western Australia and Northern Territory. They are barbaric systems of punishment and I cannot understand how our Prime Minister can sit on his hands when kids are being hauled into prison for stealing food, textas or cordial. It's a national shame and I support the United Nations in their attempts to pressure Howard to act, to allow a conscience vote by others in his government to overturn the law, just as occurred with the Northern Territory's euthanasia laws. What the authorities should be looking at is *why* the kids stole the things in the first place. To throw kids in prison, thinking to hell with the reasons behind their 'crimes', is sinful.

I found my time in Brisbane when I played for the Broncos in 1997 very frustrating. While I arrived in the northern capital with high expectations, the Queensland police saw me as what they call 'another black bastard'. One night, I'll never forget the humiliation, I was pulled over *three* times in the space of an hour. Three times! By the third I was a mess. I was crying, I was angry. But mostly the incidents confirmed to me that we Aborigines are considered the lowest of the low. To the cops our status is so poor it's beyond the realms of possibility that an Aborigine can drive a flash car.

At the time I must say attitudes in Queensland were very rednecked because the state was gripped by Pauline Hanson fever and that woman's words of venom against the Aboriginal race. She called us, among many things, cannibals, and I believe she was responsible for bringing some dreadful attitudes to the surface.

As my profile has increased the police have become aware

of who I am. They've stopped pulling me over for a 'licence check' ever since I vented my fury at unfair treatment, in the *Sun Herald*.

Nevertheless, a year later, and back in Liverpool Street, Sydney, my cousin Lindsay and I were dragged from my car and into a police paddy wagon on account of our skin colour. We were both released without being charged and news of my problems created an outrage. Former Wallaby skipper Mark Ella vented his spleen, telling the press, 'It's an utter disgrace that this sort of thing can happen. People should be treated as equals. Anthony knows how to behave—he's not some kind of thug.'

OK, the police pulled me over when they caught me talking on my mobile phone while I was driving. I did the wrong thing, fair enough. However, their manner towards us was dreadful; we were spoken to as if we were dogs and I reminded the officers they were dealing with a human being. It was alleged by a constable that Lindsay stuck his finger up at them in an offensive manner. I don't know if he did or didn't; however, the cops asked Lindsay to produce some identification. When he told them he had none they ordered him into their paddy wagon and I freaked: 'Don't go in there Lindsay, don't go in there. They can't arrest you for not having ID.'

The police didn't like it one bit so they turned on me, asking for my identification, and I told them I'd be happy to oblige if they were polite. They said they didn't have to be polite and yanked me from the vehicle—and all this was happening in front of passers-by who recognised me as Anthony Mundine, the footballer. The cops were quite forceful and I told them to relax, they didn't need to get rough.

Lindsay and I were only in the wagon for a few minutes before a different police officer released us. They'd looked up their computers and found out who they were dealing with. I have no doubt my profile saved me from a night in the cells. Unfortunately other Aborigines don't have that safety valve and they're left at the mercy of the lawmen.

Dad knew what I was living with in regards to all this. While he has chosen to live a quiet life he was concerned for me and came out punching when he told the *Daily Telegraph* he was concerned I had become a target for the police. 'I feel sorry for Anthony,' he said. 'I know what he's going through. It was the same story with me when I had a bit of money back in the early '70s. If I was ever driving around in a flashy car I'd expect to get pulled over by the cops at any time. It's obvious nothing has changed.'

And if you think you're different, you're cool, ask yourself this. Whenever you hear that two Aboriginal kids have been apprehended and held on suspicion for a crime, what's your immediate reaction? Innocent or guilty? If you said guilty, then I'm afraid things will never change for the Aborigines. Remember, everyone—even if they're black—is innocent until proven otherwise.

# CHAPTER 11

# RUNNING SCARED

*If I had the chance at Sydney and the occasion warranted it I would definitely fly the Aboriginal flag. But I won't do it just for the sake of doing it.*
Cathy Freeman on her Olympic plans, News Ltd Press, 2000

C athy Freeman is seen by white Australia as the perfect Aboriginal role model, and I wouldn't dare to disagree with their choice. She's a world champion, she talks of her pride in being an Australian *and* an Aborigine, and has drive like few others.

But while I admire her enormously, I was personally upset when she called upon Aborigines *not* to stage protests during the Sydney Olympics. Her call pierced my heart because Cathy was the person who won acclaim in 1994 from most fair-minded Australians by ignoring the repeated threats of severe repercussions by Australia's Commonwealth Games chief Arthur Tunstall when she draped the Aboriginal flag over her shoulder for the 200 metres victory lap in Victoria, Canada. What hurt, what really got me going, was remembering how I once sat down and spoke to Cathy about my hopes and dreams for our people. I told her I wanted to be like Ali and not only be a great athlete, but also a person who helped to prick his nation's conscience about the treatment and the plight of the downtrodden. Cathy's advice for me was to 'speak from the heart'. I do. And when Cathy wrote in her News Limited syndicated column during the buildup to the Sydney Olympics that she had no intention of being 'political' at the 2000 Games, I told the press what upset me most of all about Cathy's 'plea' was my thinking they were her words or sentiments.

I now reckon, however, that either the head honchos from SOCOG or the Olympic Federation, or even Federal Government members had a word in Cathy's ear and messed with her mind. Cathy's become too big and the people who run the country realise she's a threat because she has won the public over. In fact, they're terrified. They realise it is important to have their friends close to them and their enemies even closer, and I believe Cathy has been won over with awards such as Australian of the Year. The results of their efforts were printed in bold black type in the News Limited papers. The words, which are supposed to have come from Cathy's mouth, read in part like this:

> Leading up to the Olympics much will be made about me being an Aborigine . . . but I am not at the Olympics to be political . . . I am at the Olympic Games to run the fastest 400m of my life. Calls for an Aboriginal boycott of the Olympics frustrate me . . . There is more to gain by Cathy Freeman being on the world stage representing the Aboriginal people . . . I understand there are people very angry at the way my people were treated . . . but now is the time to work together for a better future.

Her words were a major setback for the Aboriginal activists who warned the government of mass protests throughout the Olympics, but I took heart, believing she would do something to highlight such issues as deaths in custody, the unacceptable youth suicide rate, the deplorable living conditions, lousy job prospects and the poor health of our people. If Cathy cut loose and spoke her mind, I'm willing to bet she would make it clear she doesn't want the next generation of Aboriginal children to endure the hardships which have plagued ours and the ones which preceded us.

I was so desperate for a statement of sorts to be made during the Games because I believe the Olympics is the only genuine stage where people can express their feelings on matters of far greater importance than gold medals and world records. Indeed, some of the Olympic Games' most magic moments in the past have centred on those athletes who stood up for their beliefs in the face of immense pressure. In the Berlin Games in 1936, for instance, the great black American athlete Jesse Owens made a mockery of Adolph Hitler's belief in the superiority of the Arian race; Muhammad Ali threw the gold medal he won at the Rome Olympics into a river after he was called a 'nigger' on his return to the US; and thirty-two years ago in Mexico, Tommie Smith and John Carlos entered the history books when they saluted Black Power.

Perhaps it was selfish of me to hope Cathy would do something which would floor everyone, but I do take exception when people ask what has been my statement; what has been my show of solidarity. Well, I walked away from a $600,000 NRL contract because I believed that in a society based on free enterprise, rejecting the big bucks of League because I couldn't handle its racism anymore was the biggest statement I could make at that time.

I started this chapter on Cathy Freeman by saying I admire her. And despite my personal disappointment in her decision to push the Aboriginal issue to the back of her mind, it is my hope she enjoys great success and happiness in her life. Cathy has made an impact on everyday people. She's run into their lives. Once, in a newspaper interview, the girl from Mackay, North Queensland, gave the impression she was an accidental hero:

I figure as I grow older I realise that [the responsibility of being a role model] is a bit of an added pressure, but if I can help without really meaning to help people then I think that's great. It's a gift to be able to reach into and affect people's lives. It's a wonderful thing to be able to enter people's lives, and it's not something I take for granted . . . not at all. I appreciate it but I don't take it too seriously. I have lived life before I was Cathy Freeman and I was very happy. You can take all that away and I am still going to be happy.

And I hope she always is.

# CHAPTER 12

# ABORIGINAL ACHIEVERS

As you know by now, I have no doubt some influential members of white Australia want the rest of the world to picture the average Aborigine as a layabout who spends their time stretched under a tree and stoned off their face from cheap wine or illicit drugs. I say that because I figure the idea that we're more inclined to waste our lives than strive for success makes it that little bit easier for them to justify the atrocities which have been committed against my people over the last 200 years. The idea that Aborigines are a lazy, good-for-nothing race has been bred into the white culture since Phillip first set foot in Australia in 1778, and has been quickly embraced by some other nationalities who have followed in the post-war immigration boom. Non-Anglo-Saxon Australians are just as inclined to tell jokes about us, like the one about Jesus Christ telling the Aborigines to do nothing until he came back.

Nevertheless, Australian history is crammed with Aborigines who have got up off their backsides and made something of themselves. They include activist Charles Perkins; politician Neville Bonner; magistrate Pat O'Shane; Rugby League players Arthur Beetson, John Ferguson, Ricky Walford and Larry Corowa; Olympic gold medallist Nova Perris-Kneebone; the poet Oodgeroo Nunukul; and actress Deborah Mailman. They are just some who have made their name in the white bloke's world, and—even though I have made my name as an Aboriginal sportsman—I find myself imploring the next generation of

Aborigines not to look at their fists or feet as their ticket into 'acceptability'. I again urge them to hit the schoolbooks and become educated. I believe our people have a greater need for Aboriginal doctors, schoolteachers, lawyers and dentists than we do for footballers, boxers and athletes. Besides, it isn't as though we don't already have our role models to draw strength from when our personal challenges become too much. There is an army of them—and I'm proud to present my pick of those Aborigines who have made an impact on modern Australia, ranging from opera singers to artists to soldiers.

## THE GREAT MUNDINE
### Anthony (Tony) William Mundine M.B.E.
### World Boxing Title contender
### Born: 1951

*Maybe they will stop and think that if Tony can become a champion in the white world, so can I . . .*
TONY MUNDINE ON SUCCESS

At the peak of my father's boxing career, Aborigines from all over the country would leave the shantytowns they lived in and drive to Sydney or Brisbane to cheer him. Many would arrive in cars he'd bought them years before with money he made in the ring. Dad was a hero to our people. They were well aware he started his life in a one-room humpy made of packing cases and corrugated iron, and rose to become the leading contender for the mighty Carlos Monzon's world middleweight crown.

History notes that Dad had no hope against Monzon. The Argentinian not only ranks with Sugar Ray Leonard as the world's greatest middleweight, but as the Sydney newspaper columnist Jeff Wells once pointed out, he liked to fight in his own backyard—and with his own referees. When my brave Dad locked horns with him, Monzon hadn't suffered a defeat in ten long years and, while Dad was well in the hunt for the opening six rounds, the Argentinian stepped up a gear in the seventh and destroyed my father's world title dream with a volley of vicious punches. Nevertheless, the name Tony Mundine rates with those of Les Darcy, Lionel Rose, Vic Patrick and Jeff Fenech as one of this nation's greatest fighters.

Even so it burns me to think few other fighters had to endure the insults and guffaws of beer-gutted journalists and wannabes perched on their bar stools. They jibed him about a supposed glass jaw; they said he had no heart. But I tell you they were dead wrong. Not only did Tony Mundine wear the Commonwealth middleweight and light-heavyweight crowns, but he was the Australian champion from the middle to heavyweight divisions. No Aussie, white or black, was good enough to beat him and even one of his archrivals, Charkey Ramon, thanked his lucky stars that he was spared a fight against Dad because of a career-ending injury. 'Everybody wanted the fight to go on,' he said, 'but I'm quite happy I didn't get into the ring with him. Tony is a big, strong boy.'

I believe my father's frame was better suited for the light-heavyweight ranks and I think his having to shed pounds to make the lighter division's weight limit went against him; it sapped him of energy in important fights. However, Dad has long believed it was a matter of timing. He told Larry Writer in the book *Winning* he went for the early kill and would start building up a few days before. When the bell went he'd explode into the ring, slip his opponent's punches and make him miss three or four times, then hit him with a shock punch. Dad noted there was a pattern in his career that he'd win a major fight against a world-class boxer, then in his next bout, often against an average fighter, he'd relax and struggle. Once or twice he got knocked out by nobodies.

But after beating the former world welterweight and middle-weight champion Emille Griffiths in Paris, the French took Dad to their hearts, and it pleases me no end to be told that in gyms around France there are hung fading black and white photographs of my father in his prime.

Dad earned an estimated $500,000 out of boxing, but nothing quite matched the joy he gained from buying my grandparents a home in the respectable Sydney suburb of Earlwood. 'It made fifteen years of boxing worthwhile,' he proudly told the media.

By the time he retired from the ring in 1983 Dad had fought ninety-six times, scored eighty wins (sixty-five by KO), was stopped ten times and lost five decisions. He was tempted to make a comeback in 1990 to help the then World Boxing Council title, but his offer was refused by his trainer, Manny Hinton. This angered Dad and reinforced that even at thirty-nine years old he would be a threat to the younger boxers who were making good money. 'When it comes to speed, punching power and timing,' he growled, 'I'm just as good as the blokes going around now.'

While he had been inspired by George Foreman's efforts to win twenty from as many in his comeback, Dad shelved those plans, including a shot at the World Boxing Federation's title in Beijing in the early 1990s.

But even these days he's still fighting—for his people. Dad became a troubleshooter for the Federal Department of Aboriginal Affairs, tackling the problems of alcoholism, drug abuse and juvenile crime within the Aboriginal community—and he put his heart and soul into it. And with his gymnasium in Eveleigh Street he is trying his best to teach Aboriginal and other kids that there is more to life than drugs, drink and crime. As I've said, he forbids swearing in the gym and I can only say that anyone who was stupid enough to try to push drugs in that place wouldn't know what hit them.

Dad has also broken the cycle which seems to affect many successful Aboriginal boxers. He hasn't been KO-ed by the bottle and rather than get intoxicated by the backslaps, he's managed to be a success long after hanging up his well-worn gloves.

But the list of Aboriginal fighters who have finished in the gutter is a sorry—if little-read—chapter in Australian sporting history. Australia's first Aboriginal champion, Jerry Jerome from Dalby, in the Queensland outback, was a freak. In the big-bellied boxer's first big fight against the Frenchman Ercole de Balzac he crawled out on all fours and mimicked an ape before belting the startled Frenchman with a volley of sting lefts and rights. When de Balzac blazed back, Jerome sprang high into the air like a ballet dancer and ran around the ring making faces at the shocked Frenchman before he ended it with a left hook in the fifth round. In other fights he used what he called the Devil Dance of the Wirra tribe to psych his opponents out of the bout. After his retirement he lived at the Barambah Aboriginal Settlement (now known as Cherbourg) in squalor. It's been said that when Jerome died in 1950 he lay in bed wearing a tattered old bowler hat, his only reminder of an incredible career.

Ron Richards, a tent fighter who came close to fighting for the world title, was a proud boxer who used his cash to buy homes in middle-class Sydney suburbs. His fists of fury also bought him respect. At a time when Aborigines weren't allowed into hotels or permitted to vote, he married a white woman, although the union did raise eyebrows and it caused problems. Ever the fighter, Richards overcame them, but he fell victim to the demon water and became a punching bag for vagrants in Sydney's Haymarket area. It's cruel to think that the man who rattled future world champions such as Gus Lesnevich and

Archie Moore was battered from pillar to post by hoboes who'd stumble over their feet in their haste to brag to their drunken mates they'd flogged the one-time hero of Sydney Stadium.

In 1947, Richards was shipped back to Queensland by train to live on Palm Island as a virtual prisoner of the Aboriginals' Protection Board. In his book *Lords of the Ring*, Peter Corris wrote Richards' epitaph when he said his career looked like a fantasy—that of a tent-fighting back-blocks Aborigine who did well financially and beat Americans and others. Corris said Richards was proof that an Aborigine could succeed in Australia and at the same time proved that the Aborigines were 'fatally flawed'.

Dad, however, has proven we can succeed in and out of the ring. And while Tony Mundine has never sought approval or accolades from anyone, least of all me, when he was once asked how he'd like to be remembered, he said: 'I hope people remember me as an Aborigine who got off his backside and did his best. A bloke who got up and had a go.'

As far as I'm concerned, Dad doesn't need a belt to be rated a world champion.

## ROSE AGAINST THE ODDS
**Lionel Edmund Rose M.B.E.**
**World boxing champion**
**Born: 1948**

Such was Lionel Rose's drawing power when he reigned supreme that the great American rock 'n' roll star Elvis Presley would wear a false beard and dark glasses to watch him strut his stuff in the boxing rings around Los Angeles. Rose's explosiveness and grace were so majestic the prestigious *London Times* described him as Australia's first world champion since the great Aboriginal artist Albert Namatjira.

CHAPTER 12 - Aboriginal Achievers

CHAPTER 12 - Aboriginal Achievers

His king of the world status in 1968 was a far cry from his upbringing in a one-room shanty in the Aboriginal settlement Jackson's Track, five kilometres up the dirt road from the Gippsland township of Drouin. Like me, boxing was in Lionel's blood. His father Roy was a tent fighter and he taught his son the noble art in a ring made from fencing wire stretched between gum trees. Unfortunately for Lionel, his father wasn't ringside when he had his first fight at Melbourne's famous Festival Hall. He had dropped dead of a heart attack at the age of thirty-four and his wife Gina was left with the tough job of raising nine kids on her own. Rose attended his father's funeral in the morning and lost his bout for the Victorian flyweight title later that night.

At nineteen Rose was given his shot at immortality against the great Japanese world champion Fighting Harada and, despite his being a 4–1 underdog, Rose was confident he could beat the veteran of fifty-four tough pro fights in Tokyo. The Japanese sportswriters dubbed him the Black Kangaroo and they delighted in hearing the reason Lionel smoked a pipe was because it was an ancient Aboriginal aid to physical fitness. But the laughter ended on the night of the fight. With three Japanese judges sitting ringside, Rose was told towards the end of the fight by his manager Jack Rennie: 'No more boxing. You must punch it out. Hit him twice every time he hits you.' This, Lionel did, and when the unanimous decision in his favour was announced he leapt into the arms of Rennie like a baby joey and the pair crashed to the canvas laughing like kids.

Rose returned to a tremendous turnout; 250,000 people lined the streets of Melbourne's Central Business District to salute a great Aboriginal hero.

However, as is the way with boxing, Lionel fell on hard times. It's estimated he made and spent half a million dollars and his reason for doing so was a typical Aboriginal cry: 'When life is a battle you spend your money, what the hell.' In his declining years the media called him an 'easybeat' when he lost fights, and then a 'dead beat' when he was arrested while hiding in a classroom trying to steal a school's video recorder. Lionel made unwanted headlines a second time when he was imprisoned for eight days after being caught for driving while disqualified. But rather than disappear into an ocean of mediocrity, Lionel—the Man's man—picked himself up to get a job with the Department of Aboriginal Affairs as an inspiration for kids in both remote outposts and suburbs of inner-city squalor. Twenty years after Rose's fairytale ride to the top, and his defeat of Harada, Channel Seven turned his remarkable life into a multimillion-dollar miniseries, reinforcing my belief that anyone from anywhere, even a dirt-floored humpy in outback Victoria, can make it if they get a lucky break.

**CRICKET'S BLACK OPAL**
**Eddie Gilbert**
**Queensland Sheffield Shield cricketer**
**Born: 1908 Died: 1978**

*. . . the ball came through at bewildering speed . . .*
*accentuated because Gilbert only shuffled about four quick*
*steps before delivering the ball. One ball knocked the bat out of*
*my hand, and I unhesitatingly class this short burst as [equal*
*to] anything seen from [bodyline bowler] Harold Larwood or*
*anyone else . . .*
SIR DONALD BRADMAN IN HIS AUTOBIOGRAPHY *FAREWELL TO CRICKET*,
PAVILIONS, LONDON, 1988.

When I first saw Andrew Symonds play for the Australian One Day Cricket team my immediate thought was that he had to be twice as good as everyone else in the national team because while he isn't an Aborigine he seems to have some dark blood in him. I say that because, despite their recent attempts to make inroads into the Aboriginal community, Australian cricket doesn't have a history of promoting outsiders. The tragic story of Eddie Gilbert has helped shape such a belief.

Gilbert was taken from his mother's arms when he was just four years old to live on the Cherbourg Aboriginal settlement in Queensland under the supervision of the Protector of Aborigines. It was there he was introduced to cricket, the sport used by the engineers of the British Empire to 'civilise' the natives in far-flung outposts like India, Ceylon, South Africa, the Caribbean and Australia. The game quickly took hold in the Australian colonies and, while it was predominantly a white man's sport, it's interesting to think the first Australian team to tour 'motherland' England in 1868 consisted entirely of Aborigines! And, between 1824 and 1908, a time when 10,000 Aborigines were butchered in Queensland, people would flock from the nearby township of Ipswich to watch the Aborigines play cricket at Deebing Creek. The *Queensland Times* even wrote that they 'behaved like white gentlemen—indeed, they were a noble example'. And then they'd go and kill them. (While some Aborigines gained a begrudging acceptance among the whites, it's sad to think Tasmania's first Aboriginal cricketer, Shiney or Shinal, was beheaded on his death and his skull sent to an Irish museum for preservation.)

Gilbert didn't take long to make an impact in the South Burnett and Gympie competitions, and while he didn't enjoy too many big scores in the First Class arena, he belted Bradman-type knocks in the Queensland backblocks with 210 and 120 (retired). However, it was as a lightning-quick bowler that he caught the attention of the game's hierarchy, and from 1930 to 1931 Gilbert made his debut for the Queensland Sheffield Shield team. He enjoyed tremendous results, including his five wickets for sixty-five runs and two for twenty-six against the visiting West Indies. A touching sidelight during the match was Gilbert congratulating the West Indies master blaster Learie Constantine for hitting a mighty six off his bowling.

Then he bowled his way into history when he dismissed the mighty Bradman for what Sir Donald himself called the 'luckiest duck' of his career. Earlier in the over Gilbert removed Bradman's cap with a bouncer which so unbalanced him he fell to the ground. An interesting snapshot of Aboriginal defiance is the image of Gilbert standing over the pride of Australian sport, who was lying on his back.

Despite his celebrity status, Gilbert was still a black man. He was bound by the Protector of Aborigines' law and this prevented him from doing things his white team-mates took for granted. For instance, he had to ask for permission to travel to matches in a car with his Queensland team-mates. The Protector of Aborigines said Eddie couldn't live in Brisbane unless he had a proper job and was kept under strict supervision. As a result, the bowler who humbled Bradman, among others, was forced to sleep in a tent pitched in the backyard of the Queensland Cricket Board secretary's home during the season—and then he'd be shipped back to the mission after the last day's play of the season. That thought blows my mind, as it adds yet another line to the great shame that is Australia's history of race relations.

While there have been suggestions Gilbert was ignored for a baggy green cap because of his ebony skin, others are adamant he was overlooked because he had a suspect bowling action—poor Eddie was dubbed a chucker by a Victorian umpire who was alleged to have had a reputation of no-balling all but his home state's bowlers. Gilbert was a respected member of the Queensland side and from all reports spectators all over the country appreciated his skill. Indeed, it can be taken as some sort of tribute that, in an era when most hotels had a 'NO ABORIGINES ALLOWED' edict, Eddie was welcomed everywhere he toured with the team. Indeed, he certainly fared much better than Johnny Mullagh, who played for Victoria in the 1870s. When he was told by an innkeeper that a room next to the stables was good enough for a 'nigger', Mullagh, a gentle man, opted to sleep in the open yard as his quiet protest.

While Gilbert was called a 'chucker' by the 'lily-whites' another Aborigine, Jack Marsh, was overlooked for a test berth as a 'chucker' despite being rated by the English tourists in 1904 as the world's fastest bowler. And even though Gilbert's later years were downright tragic in themselves, Marsh was battered to death by two whites in a street fight outside a billiard hall in western New South Wales just twelve years after he was the world's most feared bowler. The judge acquitted the two men, saying the dead man might have deserved the kicking he received while he lay on the ground.

When Victorian umpire Barlow no-balled Gilbert from square leg he was hooted by the Melbourne crowd and told to get off the field because they thought his ruling was unfair. And while the mob's reaction was supported by the cameras which filmed his action at just about every angle, no-one could find a flaw except for the national selectors who kept him out of the test team. This was in spite of such supporters as star batsman Archie Jackson, who, at the height of the 'chucking' furore, wrote, 'The adulation he has received has not affected his equilibrium. Such a player is an ornament to the game; may he continue to prosper.'

Sadly, Eddie didn't prosper. The chucker controversy chased him out of cricket and, in 1937, he played his last game for the Maroons. But even though Eddie Gilbert did not wear the baggy green cap, he did something even greater. Apart from forcing his way into the 'gentleman's' game of cricket, he gave all Aborigines heart when he dismissed Bradman for a duck! Indeed, Dr Ken Edwards, who spent six years researching Gilbert, summed up the fast bowler's life when he said that even though Gilbert was acclaimed by the masses, he was still incarcerated in a settlement.

The authorities had carefully cultivated the public image of a clean living, non-drinking black. But Gilbert's private life was rife with problems and in 1948 he was admitted to the Goodna Mental Asylum suffering congenital syphilis—a disease which was rampant among Aborigines at the time. The boy who was forced from the arms of his mother to live on a mission when he was only four years old and then enjoyed a brief moment of social acceptance when he removed Bradman for a duck, stayed there until his death in 1978. Eddie Gilbert is remembered as only one of a handful of Aborigines to have played first class cricket and I'm sure that, despite his being snubbed by the test selectors, he'd be proud to think that Jason Gillespie, who recently revealed he has some tribal blood, went one step further and represented Australia.

## LADY ACE
**Evonne Cawley (nee Goolagong)**
**Tennis champion**
**Born: 1951**
*Evonne's such a child, such a nature's child.*
TED TINLING ON EVONNE GOOLAGONG

When Evonne Goolagong turned eleven she left her home to live with a white family—but, unlike thousands of other Aboriginal kids, it was at the will of her parents. Rather than being dragged away kicking and screaming by officers of the court she was sent from the New South Wales country town of Barellan to Sydney to make the most of her extraordinary tennis skills. She was sent to live with renowned tennis coach Vic Edwards and his family. He became Evonne's legal guardian when she turned fourteen and he helped put her on the road to fame and fortune.

In a six-year period Evonne won thirty-seven junior national titles, a success which helped prepare her to conquer the tennis world with a rare poise and grace. While her critics say lapses in Evonne's concentration meant she didn't dominate world tennis as she should have, she won hearts all over the world—and she also won plenty of trophies. In thirteen glorious years she won ninety-two professional tournaments, including Wimbledon (twice), the Australian Open (four times) and the Italian, South African, French and US Indoor Open titles. More importantly, however, she was a great ambassador for her people.

In 1980 Evonne created history by becoming the first mother since Dorothy Chalmers to come back and win Wimbledon when she defeated the robot-like Chris Evert-Lloyd in two sets, nine years after her first Wimbledon triumph. In an age where the game was dominated by the mechanical manner of Ivan Lendal and the tantrums of John McEnroe, Evonne added her grace and ladylike manner. It made her one of the world's most popular athletes and, from an Aborigine's perspective, she proved that a little girl with a dream can climb mountains. My people watched in awe as the kid from Barellan progressed from being a five-year-old girl who liked to bash a ball against a wall of the family home to being rated the world's number one player in 1975. Evonne's was the only Aboriginal family in Barellan, but it wasn't until her mother's death in 1971 that she realised she didn't know much about her Aboriginality and set about learning all she could about the ways of her ancestors.

She became the first Aborigine to sit on the Board of the Australian Sports Commission, and she has encouraged more Aboriginal children to play sport and embrace a healthy lifestyle. And she is trying to show them how to do it with her trademark style and grace.

## MUSOS WITH SOUL
## Yothu Yindi
## Northern Territory rock group

*Yothu Yindi is the flagship of the Australian Musical Movement . . .*

*BILLBOARD*

Through their music Yothu Yindi have given every Aborigine a voice on the world stage. While their music and dance reflects the deep spiritual link the Yolnga people of North-East Arnhem Land have with the earth and the creatures which live on it, they also tell of my people's plight—the loss of culture, our 'dead' languages, and the feelings of a people who have lost their land. And, brother, they put it to a mean beat. While the band sings of its hopes for a truly united Australia, they also provide prayers for the environment and they urge our generation, regardless of skin colour, to embrace conservation and stop scarring the face of Mother Earth before it's too late.

The yidaki (didgeridoo) and other traditional instruments such as the bilma (wooden clapping sticks) provide the band with its distinctive sound, while their passion gives their music terrific soul. But despite their outstanding success the group has proven you don't need to sell your soul to do well. Yothu Yindi has remained faithful to the tribe's sacred rituals, which the lead singer, Mandawy Yunupingu, made clear when he told a journalist: 'I'll never betray them . . . we think of ourselves as Yolnga, first and always.'

Yothu Yindi recorded their first album *Homeland Movement* in white Australia's bicentennial year, 1988, and the job was completed in one day. Their ability to marry Western music with the traditional music of the Gumatyi and Rirratjingai clans of Arnhem Land was considered good enough to gain them a record deal. It provided them with the opportunity to reach the international audience with their groundbreaking song 'Treaty', which not only spent twenty-two weeks in the national Top 20, but was also the first song in an Aboriginal language to enjoy extensive airplay here and abroad.

The band has also gone on the road to help highlight the Aboriginal cause, touring Papua New Guinea, New Zealand, Germany, France, the Netherlands, Belgium, Great Britain, Canada, the US, Brazil and Africa—and they lay 'em in the aisles. I reckon they deserve to be regarded as one of Australia's most successful acts and a lot of their achievement is due to the lead singer Mandawy Yunupingu—he's an inspiration! Now close to sixty, the former Australian of the Year boasts a Bachelor of Education which he did via correspondence. He's the principal of the Yirrakala Aboriginal Primary School and, as someone who was raised in the era when priests and missionaries tried to save the Aborigine's supposed 'black' soul, he is encouraging his students—and his own six kids—to embrace the traditional ways. It's one way to at least keep the remnants of our culture alive.

# THE MAN

**BLACK FACE IN A SLOUCH HAT**
**Captain Reginald Walter Saunders**
**Soldier, Australian Imperial Force**
**Born: 1920 Died: 1990**

*There's a lot to be proud about. And you stand out. I was a reasonable footballer, but I got a lot more votes in best-and-fairest awards than I deserved, because umpires noticed me. Nah, cobber . . . I wouldn't be white for quids.*

REG SAUNDERS ON BEING AN ABORIGINE IN A WHITE MAN'S ARMY, THE BULLETIN

While I am vehemently opposed to war, the achievements of Reg Saunders in becoming the only Aborigine to be commissioned in the Australian armed services during World War II were groundbreaking. He was giving orders to white men at a time when Aborigines were considered inferior; they couldn't vote, they required a special permit to buy alcohol, and at the beginning of the war, in 1939, non-Europeans were told they need not apply for military service.

Saunders, however, didn't see himself as a black man. He was first and foremost an infantryman and he saw service in Greece, Crete and Papua New Guinea. He also proved Aborigines could succeed in a white environment, even one as regimented as the military. He was blessed with plenty of gumption, too. When the German forces overran Crete and forced many of the allied soldiers to either surrender to the Nazis or take refuge in the mountains, the warrior from the Wannan tribe took his chances in the hills. He and four other Aussies avoided being captured, by living off their wits and thanks to the kindness of the Greeks.

On one occasion, when he had taken refuge in a Greek cafe, a patrol of Germans entered it for a coffee. Rather than panic, the black-skinned Saunders walked up to the enemy and asked

108

them for cigarettes. The Germans drank their coffee and swallowed his bluff. He eventually escaped the island on a British trawler and returned to Australia to help fight off his country's second invasion—this time by the Japanese. (His brother Harry, who also showed great leadership qualities, was killed fighting the Japanese at Gona in 1942.)

In 1944, General Blamey, the commander of the AIF, approved Saunders' promotion to the rank of lieutenant and he gained the universal respect of his men. However, at the end of the war, Saunders returned to civilian life and the shadows of obscurity. The man who was saluted on parade grounds struggled to find work and was refused service in hotels because of the colour of his skin. One time, when he was refused service by a Sydney barmaid because of the laws, he showed the same wit which helped him fool Adolf Hitler's troops in the cafe. Saunders told her he was an Indonesian student. She apologised and poured him a drink. On other occasions, when he was pestered by white drunks who wanted to tell him about their service with the legendary black officer Reg Saunders, he'd reply, 'Saunders? I never heard of him.'

He rejoined the military at the outbreak of the Korean War and while he was fighting the Chinese in the Battle of Kapyong his wife and children were living in one room of a rat-infested, condemned house. According to his biographer, Harry Gordon, the captain remained tolerant of those who displayed intolerance towards him.

Saunders wasn't the only Aborigine who served in the military—Aborigines have served in the Australian army since the Boer War at the turn of the 20th century. While thousands of black Australians were prepared to risk their lives on foreign battlefields for a country that has never really appreciated them, they encountered prejudice of all sorts, none less than when actually being accepted at the enlistment centre. The Universal Training Scheme in the Defence Act of 1909 meant Aborigines were excluded from military service and it was due to the shortage of volunteers towards the end of World War II that the ban was relaxed. And while 400 Aborigines defied the colour ban to fight on the battlefields of World War I—many claimed to be Maori—they returned only to remain without voting rights, citizenship or even the pension afforded to white veterans! In 1939, the honorary secretary of the Aborigines' League, William Cooper, who lost a son in World War I, penned his protest to the government:

> The Aboriginal has no status, no rights, no land and though the native is more loyal to the person of the King and the throne than the average white he has no country and nothing to fight for but the privilege of defending the land which was taken from him by the white race without compensation or even kindness.

The Aborigines proved their courage, and they gained respect and friendship from their white comrades—in many cases those bonds extended into life after the military. One, a full-blooded warrior from Warrnambool, William Rawlings, led an attack on a German Communications trench at Morian Court, France, and was recommended for the Military Medal. Another, Benno Murray, fought at Gallipoli. John Arthur Firebrace and Harry Thorpe (a Military Medal recipient) are buried at Heath Cemetery, Harbonnieres, France. The list goes on. William Chatfield, from Burra Bee Dee Mission, Coonabarabran, joined the legendary Light Horse Brigade and helped to write one of the most glorious chapters in Australia's military history—the charge of Beersheeba.

One dark digger, Private Douglas Grant, was captured by

Germans at Bullecourt, France, and the French were excited about having a member of the world's oldest race in their midst. Grant was only two when his parents were killed in a punitive raid in 1887 and he was raised by a white man who adopted him. He enlisted in 1916 but was removed from the troopship and discharged from the army because of the regulations which prevented Aborigines leaving the country without government permission. Despite that insult he re-enlisted a few months later. But his war ended when he was captured and sent to the Wunsdorf prisoner of war camp near Berlin. Grant became an object of curiosity among anthropologists in Berlin. They studied him, measured his skull, took photographs, made a bust of him and asked questions about the Aboriginal race. I can imagine one would might have been, 'Why the hell are you fighting?'

In World War II Aborigines and Torres Strait Islanders served in the military, worked as labourers, formed guerilla groups and made other sacrifices—like not lighting their cooking fires along the coast near Darwin because of the threat of Japanese bombing raids. Unlike the white volunteers the Aborigines were paid in rations and given some pocket money. It wasn't until most of them had died off that the government, in 1991, gave them and their next of kin back pay.

While Reg Saunders became the first Aborigine to be given a commission, Leonard Waters became the first Aboriginal fighter pilot. He flew ninety-two sorties against the Japanese and made others at Tobruk, El Alamein, the Pacific and Papua New Guinea. And while many paid the ultimate price it's disgusting to realise people like the former Queensland premier Sir Joh Bjelke Petersen are oblivious to the contribution Aborigines made to this country. On one occasion, speaking of the American efforts to help defend Australia, he sounded as if no Aborigine had fought for their country. 'The Aborigine people would not be here today if it was not for the United States of America who fought the Battle of the Coral Sea,' he said. Sadly, brother, gratitude is at the whim of the recipient of good deeds.

**ELLA MAGIC**
**Mark, Glen and Gary Ella**
**Australian Rugby Union players**
*In 1977, they were chosen in the Australian Schoolboys team to [go to] Great Britain, a significant tour, not only because the team remained undefeated but because it gave the rest of the Rugby world a first glimpse of the young Ellas.*
IAN HEADS AND GARY LESTER, *200 YEARS OF AUSTRALIAN SPORT*, ANGUS & ROBERTSON, SYDNEY, 1988

The world-acclaimed Ella brothers grew up in a household of twelve siblings near the shores of Botany Bay. From playing thousands of backyard 'tests' they developed a unique running style which catapulted Mark, Gary and Glen to Rugby greatness.

Indeed, Mark created history when he became the first Aborigine to captain the Wallabies, and while he proved to be a popular captain the thing he and his brothers are most remembered for is their 'ESP' which allowed them to do the impossible on the paddock. It seemed Mark didn't need to look to see where one of his brothers was about to offload a pass. Few, even Argentina's great stand-off Hugo Porta, could thwart it and the brothers' offering to Rugby is still known as 'Ella Magic'.

Regretfully, Mark retired at his peak in 1986 to concentrate on making his name in the business world. Even though he was acclaimed as one of the Wallabies' greatest players, there were numerous offers for him to switch codes and for a while it appeared as if he would follow team-mate Michael O'Connor's lead and join my old club, St George. It's a pity he didn't because I believe the thirteen-man game would have suited him. He might have even overshadowed Wally Lewis as that era's best player. But he packed the boots away and opted for the business world. These days his company, Horton-Ella, specialises in sports management and promotions, and Mark helps to look after the West Indies cricket team, among a host of high-profile clients. A gentleman, he and his brothers are hailed as tremendous role models for the Aboriginal race wherever they go.

## CAMEL BOY WITH TALENT
## Albert Namatjira
## Landscape artist
## Born:1902 Died: 1959

*Come back, Albert Namatjira, all is forgiven . . . for being black, for sharing your grog with your mates, for getting your paintings on biscuit tins and tea trays and for making us feel ashamed and confused.*

PETER WARD, THE *AUSTRALIAN*, 1986

A few Aborigines who play top grade football in the National Rugby League are tremendous artists. They include Penrith's Sid Domic and the Wests Tigers' McGuinness brothers, Ken and Kevin. But I think few artists—black or white—match Albert Namatjira, who brought the wonder and beauty of Central Australia to life on canvas.

Namatjira, a member of the Aranda people, was born at the Lutheran Mission of Hermannsburg 300 kilometres west of Alice Springs. While the church helped protect Albert and his kind from the racial prejudices of the white pastoralists and police, they didn't allow them to practise their traditional ways of life. They segregated the families and locked the girls in dormitories after sunset for their 'moral' protection.

At thirty-two Albert was inspired to put brush to canvas when he saw the works of a Victorian artist named Rex Battarbee, who had embarked on an art tour of Central Australia in 1934. He wanted to gauge the reaction of the Aborigines to his work to see if he had captured the true spirit of the 'Dead Centre'. While most at the Lutheran Mission shouted excitedly at the places they recognised, Albert Namatjira stood silent. As he viewed Battarbee's interpretation of the ancient tribal lands he told himself: 'If a white man can paint my country like that, then so can I.'

It was the first step towards a career which brought him fame, fortune and ultimately unhappiness and disillusionment. While he was fêted as a genius by most white Australians, he could never bridge the gap between the two cultures because while he was a black man at heart and lived according to tribal laws, he was also trapped in the white world where he gained money and paid taxes. He was seen as proof that a black man could make it in a society alien to him and, wearing a tailored white suit, he was presented to Queen Elizabeth during her Royal Tour in 1954. After he gave her three of his paintings Albert was asked for his impressions of the Queen and he told the press she appeared 'a nice little girl'.

At a time when Aborigines were being paid in rations for their work as stockmen and labourers, Namatjira was earning a fortune in cash for his work. But he was constantly penniless because of the Aboriginal tradition of sharing and communal living. In the tribe a man who kills a kangaroo is expected to share it with his people and it was by this same creed that Albert shared his wealth. He was also expected to share his grog, a commodity he could buy by virtue of having gained 'citizenship' as not only a mark of respect for his ability to paint the white man's way, but because the government wanted to justify taking taxes from him.

Despite his 'acceptance' he could not buy a home in Alice

Springs because the locals objected to the thought of his fifty or so relatives arriving in their streets. Forced to live in a dry creek outside of town, Albert would pay a taxi driver $50 a day to deliver a few gallons of water to him. As a citizen he developed a quick taste for wine and beer and with each drinking binge his art began to disintegrate and his weight began to increase. He bloated to 115 kilos and ignored medical advice to lose weight. He also ignored the white man's law which forbade him from sharing his liquor with his tribe. So, at the risk of imprisonment, he shared it—gallons of it. Then, in 1958, someone was murdered in a drunken affray at Namatjira's camp in Alice Springs and after their investigations the police arrested Albert for supplying liquor. He was sentenced to six months' jail but the term was reduced to three when he appealed. Despite the reduction, his son had to refrain him from grabbing a rifle on hearing the news. 'Shoot me, shoot me. Kill me. Put an end to all this!' he screamed.

On his release from prison Namatjira resumed painting, but on 7 August 1959, he collapsed, suffering a heart attack, and died two days later in Alice Springs Hospital. Namatjira's greatness in death is that he made white Australia examine its conscience and wonder about the way in which he had been treated. Whitefellas had expected him to live by two completely different sets of laws. On Albert's death, one of his white friends, author Frank Clune, told the *Sunday Mirror*:

I'll always believe old Albert died of a broken heart. The public servants finally got him down. I'm not very proud to be a big, 100-per-cent Australian white man tonight. Albert was one of the whitest men I ever knew and it didn't do him much good.

Albert Namatjira's grave is marked by a mighty granite headstone which bears a quotation from the Bible in Arunta. It sums up the life of all Aborigines: 'By the Grace of God, I am because I am'.

**A LION-HEARTED DINGO**
**Ernie Dingo**
**Actor and comedian**
**Born: 1956**
Having starred alongside such Hollywood heroes as Bryan Brown and Paul Hogan, Ernie Dingo is rightly regarded as Australia's leading Aboriginal actor. I reckon his smile is just as famous as his delivery, and whenever I see Ernie Dingo strut his stuff on the television and silver screen I can't help but think that the grim face of black determination can afford a grin. While I am confrontational, Ernie prefers to be subtle in the way he goes about tackling Aboriginal issues. I reckon he probably learned that from his mum when he was a schoolboy subjected to racist remarks for receiving a government subsidy for his textbooks and fees. One day he asked his mother: 'Why is it that the government pays us money? Do they want us to be like whitefellas?' To which she replied: 'It's just because we don't have enough money to teach them to be the same as Yamatjis [Aborigines].'

Ernie has done a lot for our people and, while he's applauded by critics, he has made it clear his childhood hero wasn't a cricketer or a footballer. Instead he idolised a Kimberley Aboriginal warrior who tried to repel the great European land grab towards the turn of the 20th century. Dingo used silence as his weapon against the One Nation leader Pauline Hanson when she divided Australia with her extreme views in the late 1990s. Rather than get in a public slanging match with the redheaded Celt from Ipswich, Dingo kept his thoughts to himself. However, of the hundreds upon thousands of Australians who accepted her views, Dingo told the *Age* newspaper:

> Australians can be arrogant bastards at times. People are sick of Liberal and Labor and all their promises. Now, it's like you handle a mob of sheep. You put a leader in front and they will follow. I look at things from a bush point of view. I won't rubbish the woman. I don't want to get into an argument with her. I want to conserve my positive energy for elsewhere.

And as if to prove he inherited his mother's logic, Dingo added: 'From the Aboriginal point of view we do hear good things about Pauline Hanson. It's just that she's asleep at the time.'

Ernie Dingo is a mighty success; his smiling black face on the screen reinforces my message that Aboriginal kids don't need to look at boxing, running or football as their way out. They can aim instead for other fields—from white-collar professions to the arts. And, like Ernie, they can have fun doing it.

## THE SWEET VOICE OF BLACK DESPAIR
**Harold Blair**
**Opera singer**
**Born: 1924 Died: 1975**
*His big thing was education. He said that if Aborigine people were given the same education as white people then they could take their place in white society.*
DOCUMENTARY PRODUCER, STEVE THOMAS

While I'm more in tune with the rap singer Puff Daddy than with Pavorotti, it blows me away to think an Aborigine from Cherbourg named Harold Blair sang opera around the world. Blair successfully crossed the black/white barrier by studying at a conservatorium, marrying a white woman, living in the suburbs and being considered 'respectable' by his peers. But he never forgot his culture—and he refused to give up on his people.

Blair valued education and he campaigned strongly for Aboriginal kids to be given the same chance as European kids in the classroom. In an attempt to improve the Aborigine's lot, he initiated a program where Aboriginal kids were sent from the reservations for holidays with white families. Blair believed the two parties could learn a lot from one another and as a result of the experience a number of white people adopted Aboriginal children. Film producer Steve Thomas, who studied Blair's life, said while some of Blair's people believed he had abandoned them, he actually helped to fan the black movement in the 1950s and 1960s that culminated in the formation of the tent city in 1972.

Blair himself overcame a tragic childhood to make his mark. His fifteen-year-old mother had been raped by her stepfather and after Harold's birth they were sent to the Purga Aboriginal Mission, where they were separated by the authorities, Blair being raised in a separate dormitory. He worked as a cane-cutter, but some success in a talent quest helped put him on the bumpy road to stardom—and love.

What appeals to me about Harold Blair is he bowed to no-one, especially not to public opinion's dismay at the idea of an Aboriginal man marrying a white woman. While studying at Melbourne's Melba Conservatorium, Blair fell in love with a white mezzosoprano and they married, despite coming from two vastly different backgrounds. He had grown up as a bare-footed mission boy; she was raised in the well-to-do suburb of Camberwell. Their wedding vows made front-page news and, while some people smiled and described it as a 'breakthrough', thousands of others sneered, and said the marriage wouldn't last because of the clash of cultures.

It has been said Blair's biggest mistake was his decision to further his voice training in America rather than in the more traditional places, such as England or Italy. He didn't receive the right coaching. However, his travelling to the US allowed him to see firsthand the experiences of successful black Americans who had overcome many forms of racism to enjoy success in a number of fields. He dreamt of seeing his brothers and sisters in Australia scale such heights and he returned determined to help educate the black masses. And it was from that desire he arranged the billeting scheme. In the 1960s, he tried to provide Aborigines with their first voice in parliament when he stood for the Victorian Labor Party, but he didn't receive much support from party headquarters and lost on the preferential votes. These days, few people under fifty would know who Harold Blair is, but his achievements and his desire to help the Aboriginal race make him someone well worth honouring.

**BLACK THUNDER**
**Patrick Johnson**
**100 metre sprinter**
**Born: 1973**
*He's a very quietly spoken guy, but there's an underlying confidence about him that lets you know where he's going.*
KYLE VANDER-KUYP ON PATRICK JOHNSON

What really amazed me—as much as it annoyed me—in the lead up to the Sydney Olympics was the way in which the mainstream media overlooked the glorious achievements of Patrick Johnson in kicking Matt Shirvington's butt all over the nation. At one stage Patrick led Shirvington in their head-to-head meetings 4–0 but the telling of his efforts was restricted to just a few paragraphs; there were reams of stories written about the blond-haired, blue-eyed Shirvington's problems in remaining focused, saying things like he'd be better when he was matched against better runners! My main hope was Patrick would be afforded better treatment at the Olympics because, despite his lack of publicity, he's a mighty role model for the Aboriginal community as an individual who has mixed brawn with brains.

Raised on a mackerel trawler in Torres Strait, Patrick was discovered running at the university games when, despite no formal training, he won the 100 metres in 10.73 seconds.

Patrick had been born with a feel for speed. He saw his first ray of light when his father raced in vain to get his mother, Pearl, to the Cairns Base Hospital. Then, just two years later, Patrick's mother was killed in a car crash and her death set the scene for a childhood which could be straight from the pages of an adventure story. His youngest brother, Ryan, was sent to live with his grandma outside Cairns, while Patrick and his Irish-born father followed the wind from the Whitsundays to Torres Strait. It was on that boat the speed king learnt his formative lessons in competitiveness—in fiercely contested chess games. 'Dad used to beat me at chess when I was young. Eventually I started beating him and now he doesn't want to play any more,' he said.

While he didn't receive much formal education as a youngster—sometimes he had to swim to shore to attend his lessons—when he reached his teenage years Patrick's father sold the trawler, and the pair moved to the Southern Highlands, where he attended college to get a 'real education'. There was no stopping him.

While he loves the sensation of speed, Patrick also has a passion for languages, and from what I understand he speaks Cantonese, Mandarin, Indonesian, Japanese and his dialect of the Aboriginal language. Apart from wanting to win gold he dreams of one day working in Australia's Foreign Affairs Department— and I can't help but feel this will be tremendous for my people.

Had Patrick been inclined to grab the money and run, there is every chance we could have locked horns on the football field because in 1995 he had Canberra, North Queensland and Adelaide all trying to lure him away from the track by offering him a six figure deal. However, Patrick wanted to run. And it was my pre-Olympic hope he would run all the way to the medal winners' podium at Stadium Australia. When Johnson decided to concentrate on athletics, his Finnish coach Esa Peltola was told not to expect too much from him because like most 'Abos' he'd go 'walkabout' when the going got too tough. Through his determination and drive Patrick made his doubters eat their words—and his dust. For his part, Peltola told the press that he had met very few athletes with Patrick Johnson's iron will: 'Arto Bryggare [Finland's 1984 bronze medallist hurdler] didn't have the talent of the Americans but I never thought I would meet another athlete with the same character and commitment. Now I have,' he said of his latest pupil.

**BLACK LIKE ME**
**Nicky Winmar**
**Aussie Rules player**
**Born: 1966**
*Winmar's actions are a timely signal that it is no longer*
*acceptable for us to give tacit support to continuing racial*
*abuse from football crowds. He deserves support for his stand*
*from . . . all those who promote and broadcast Australian*
*football . . . those who have the power to influence the fans*
*should stand up and be counted on this fundamental issue.*
[EXTRACTS] LAWRIE MOLONEY, HAWTHORN
THE *SUNDAY AGE*, APRIL 1993
One of life's most defining moments for an individual who has looked the ugly face of racism square in the eye and spat at it occurred on 17 April 1993 when AFL hero Nicky Winmar

confronted a mindless mob of Collingwood supporters throwing numerous racist remarks—like 'black bastard' and worse—at him after he tangled with Magpies' rover Tony Francis. The shower of abuse heralded St Kilda's first victory over Collingwood in twenty-three years, but rather than lower himself by hurling loathsome comments at the Magpies' cheer squad, Winmar showed true grace under fire when he stood before them raising and lowering his jumper to display his black flesh. He also blew kisses at his foes. Rather than be shamed into silence, witnesses said some Magpie fans spat at the defiant Winmar as he ran towards the visitors' dressing room. But he made his point—and I love him for it.

Collingwood's president Allan McAllister added fuel to the bushfire when he reacted to the sight by saying Aboriginal footballers would gain more respect if they 'conducted themselves like white people'! It was unbelievable, and an irate Aborigine from the Top End responded to the slight by placing a curse on the Magpies—he was flown to Melbourne to lift it after they slid down the ladder towards oblivion. Look, there is no room for racism on the football field or in the grandstands, and the Winmar case cast a much-needed spotlight upon something which had previously been dismissed with a shrug of the shoulders and the comment that what happens on the paddock stays on the paddock. Indeed, I was quick to carry his torch when a Canterbury forward called me a black c*** in 1998.

While Winmar has been embroiled in numerous sporting dramas, including suspensions and fallouts with his clubs, he has often been caught in racial brawls. In 1994, Northern Territorian Aborigines were outraged when St Kilda refused to release the man called 'Cuz' for an Aboriginal All Stars game to play Collingwood in a 'reconciliation' match in Darwin. As a result of the protests Winmar was forced to apologise for a boardroom decision which was out of his hands. The sad fact of modern day sport is it's a business. Clubs invest plenty of money in their stars, which meant while the Aboriginal All Stars match against Collingwood was arranged, because of the Magpie fans who turned their acid tongues on him, St Kilda said they would not release Winmar because they were scared he might get injured. Unfortunately, the decision denied Nicky the chance to be part of an historic victory because the All Stars were too good for the AFL glamour team.

Nicky was dragged into yet another racial fistfight in 1999 when he was forced to defend himself against racist slurs by *Footy Show* host, Sam Newman. Newman took offence at Winmar's failure to turn up (because of a breakdown in communications) so he blackened his face and, with a dopey smile, told viewers that was the closest they were going to get to seeing Winmar that night. His lampooning of the wingman didn't sit well with some people, least of all Aboriginal Advancement League president Alf Bamblett, who told the *Australian*: 'It's an absolute disgrace that such a public figure could be so infantile in his behaviour. Nicky Winmar does not deserve that sort of public put-down.' Nicky demanded an apology and, while he eventually received one, a *Herald Sun* voteline poll showed an overwhelming number of readers thought Newman had done nothing wrong. And, along with a number of other Aborigines, that revelation made me wonder just how far race relations had really come.

## KYLE THE HURDLER
**Kyle Vander-Kuyp**
**Olympic hurdler**
**Born: 1971**
*At school in Mitcham in Melbourne I was the only dark kid. I remember being teased so much that one day I tried to scratch the colour from my arms . . . Mum found me and we cried together.*
KYLE VANDER-KUYP, AUSTRALIA DAY SPEECH, 2000

Kyle Vander-Kuyp says he didn't have an identity until he was a teenager and excelled at hurdles. By his own admission his background, and his life, is a mixed salad. His biological father is Irish and his mother an Aborigine, but at five weeks he was adopted by his Dutch father and white Australian mother. With that as his starting block Kyle admits it is no surprise he felt different as a child, and that was highlighted when his was the only dark face in the classroom and he was teased in the playground.

I guess Kyle was luckier than most kids from a similar background because his mother, Pat, introduced him to a number of Victoria's Aboriginal communities and she persevered with trying to get to know them, despite being initially rejected because of *her* skin colour. I was lucky to learn to be proud of my Aboriginality because of my dad, but Kyle needed a former AFL star Maurice Rioli to teach him to be proud and to use his Aboriginality as an advantage.

However, it wasn't until he joined Little Athletics that Kyle found that sense of belonging some Aborigine kids never find. Suddenly he became known as 'Kyle the hurdler' and not just 'Kyle the Abo'. And perhaps there is a message here for that army of Aboriginal people trying to find their place in the community: find something and give it your best shot because we all have potential. And, as Kyle learned, you're better off being something than nothing.

**LAST BUT NOT LEAST**
**Cathy Freeman**
**Dual world champion runner**
**Born: 1973**
One of five children, Cathy Freeman fine-tuned her ability to run like the wind by running barefoot through the bushland which surrounded her home in the North Queensland city of

Mackay. She's overcome a lot of bad things to reach the stars, including the deaths of her father and sister. However, she has conquered those terrible setbacks in the true style of a champion and run into the hearts of most Australians.

Cathy Freeman became a household name in 1994 when she won the gold medals in the 200 and 400 metres events at the Commonwealth Games and ran her victory lap by carrying both the Australian and Aboriginal flags. She was criticised by many for showing what was widely described as 'political' beliefs.

I can only dare guess the proudest person to see the Aboriginal flag flutter during those victory laps was Cathy's mother, Cecilia Barber. In 1957, Mrs Barber was a member of seven families banished from Palm Island for daring to participate in a strike against the Dickensian working conditions imposed on them by the Queensland government. In those days Palm Island was the Aboriginal race's version of Devils Island—it was a tropical hellhole where indigenous people from all over Queensland were sent for such 'crimes' as being disruptive, falling pregnant to a white man and having mixed blood.

Cathy silenced most of her remaining critics by winning even more races and in 1995 she was ranked second in the world for the 400 metres event. A year later she became the first Australian woman to not only run that distance under fifty seconds but also won the Olympic silver medal at the Atlanta Games after taking on French idol Marie-Jose Perec in what has been described as 'the greatest one-lap race of all time.' In 1997, Cathy became the world champion, a feat which was crowned by her being named Australian of the Year.

In the countdown to the Sydney Olympics, Cathy's hero status was so great she was forced to don a long black wig on a shopping expedition just so she could escape the public glare and feel 'normal' for a few hours. But ever since Cathy won her first race at age six she's been running in one direction—and that's forward. She's been blessed with the skills of her late father Norman, a popular Mackay Rugby League player who was nicknamed 'Twinkle Toes' as testimony to his blistering speed. The killer instinct hasn't come easily to Cathy. Apparently she developed it after spending many years of her childhood pulling up close to the finish line to narrow the winning margin.

While my thoughts on her running in the 2000 Olympics are well known, I appreciate her skill, courage and grace. She's a great role model and a great person. Cathy Freeman is a real winner. As an insight into the thoughts which hurtle through her mind before she launches herself from the starting blocks, she told the press in the build-up to the Sydney Olympics:

It's like you are just about to explode. It's the calm before the storm. Everything—the people you are running for, everything you live and care about, all your fears and hopes—come to this one moment. It's like you are in another place in time. It's hard to explain, but the whole universe is here now, everything you care about is here now. This is it, and you put it all there on the line and take it and use it to do the best you can because this is your time. This is what you do and I run to do the best.

# LEAGUE

# CHAPTER 13

# MAN OR MOUTH?

*Anthony Mundine is a great asset to Rugby League, the Aborigine community and all Dragon fans. He backs up his comments with a spectacular style of football and really makes everyone eat their words.*

—Renato, San Souci, the Telegraph, 17 February 2000

I have no doubt the average first grade footballer is pro-grammed to be a sterile, cliché-spitting robot who is too scared to stick his chin out and share his true character with the fans for fear of ridicule. Many of them could double as mannequins in a shopfront window. And, take it from me, most of the pulp written up in the media on a daily basis doesn't tell the true story or sum up the way most players *really* think.

To help separate fact from fiction I'll explain what the most common responses to the questions from the press *really* mean. For instance, when a player says, 'I don't care what position I play as long as I'm in first grade,' he really means, 'The coach must be kidding . . . why would he play that clown at five-eighth when I'm a better player by a mile?'. Likewise, 'I just want to make the representative team' stands for 'If I had have known I had to crawl and grovel I would have done it years ago.' And then there's the old chestnut, 'I really respect the opposition,' which means 'We're going to smash them by fifty points.' Or, 'There are seventeen players in a team and everyone is equal'; 'But if that punk rookie gets more money than me I'm out of here.' How about the desperate cry of, 'The board supports me

100 per cent'; 'They're going to knife me in the back when this dies down.' What would you prefer to read in the press? The yawn or the brawn?

As I've already said, the reason players don't share their real feelings is because they're scared—scared of being set upon by the press; scared of criticism by the club; scared of being singled out by rival supporters; scared of giving an opponent an edge. None of it worried me. I saw it as a challenge to overcome and the reason I was never scared to put obstacles in my way was because they made my feeling of accomplishment even greater. When it comes to players hyping up a big match, the NRL shouldn't be allowed to promote it as Rugby League. They should be forced, by law, to call it 'Pleasantville'! If I was a fan and heard the sanitised 'hype' I'd go watch a game of marbles before paying my hard-earned cash to see such 'intensity'.

I was a different cat to the rest; I wasn't scared to speak my mind because I not only spoke the truth but I could back up what I said. While I copped one or two hundred hidings in the media, it didn't—doesn't—worry me to let everyone know I'm The Man, and if you still doubt me look at the facts and the statistics for yourself. As far as being the game's top pivot, Laurie Daley and Brad Fittler never bettered me on the field of battle. But you didn't read that in the press because, while they loved getting a headline out of me, they became edgy when it came to paying tribute to me. However, they always seemed to have an excuse ready for those two—be it an injury, the referee or the weather.

On the subject of backing your ability, I respect the Australian test cricketer Glenn McGrath because he isn't scared to pinpoint someone like the great West Indies batsman Brian Lara on the eve of a test match and say he's going to dismiss him in both innings. While the same old dudes write their letters of outrage to the editor and make abusive calls to talkback radio hosts, saying such things would never have happened in Bradman's day, McGrath, more often than not, delivers because he knows he can. That's cool. I admire his gumption, and his much criticised aggression on the field, because sport is all about emotion, enthusiasm and entertainment.

The way I saw it, I wasn't just a footballer, I was an entertainer. I could've probably taught Sammy Davis Jnr a trick or two about showmanship, baby. People read the papers because they know I'm going to say something; they realise I'll take a stand. There's never going to be any splinters in my black butt from sitting on the fence. While many of the game's hierarchy didn't like my antics because it was supposedly American 'trash talk', judging by the reaction I've received from Rugby League fans all over Australia—and overseas—there's plenty of everyday people who get *something* out of it. For some it can be inspiration, for others it's nothing more than a bit of a laugh. But, I'll tell you this much, Rugby League won't ever fulfil its potential as a game until more players realise they're paid to *entertain* the public. We have to show our emotions—our joy and pain. As a group we have to try to touch the people outside the sidelines. They're called fans, and I'm afraid many players have lost them.

If I were a player I would look at Anthony Mundine and think to myself: 'The Man' is no fool; he's a man of absolute conviction; he's hounded by the media; a telephone book's worth of managers keep bothering him because they want to handle his affairs; he has a list of sponsors lining up for him to sign deals, and he has a strong and loyal supporter base.' If I were one of them I'd work on emancipating myself from the shackles which cripple the overwhelming majority of players. Indeed, I think the guys I played alongside and against every week should back their own ability because gagging themselves through false humility—or fear?—belies the talent and pride which has helped catapult them to the position they're enjoying. For any player daring to come out of their shell, my tip is to have commitment with a capital 'c', because if you're going to say you're the best, baby, you'd better believe it—otherwise people will carve you up at every opportunity. If you can't go that far then find something else; talk about your team and its strengths. I can find no reason why anyone would be upset by that. Oh, don't worry. Some will blame you for a loss if the team gets smashed.

I can't understand why anyone would believe their team goes out doubting their own ability, but it seems they do. A few years ago Brisbane Broncos' coach Wayne Bennett addressed his team about the reputation they were slowly but surely gaining for being 'arrogant'. He wanted them to tone it down and while most of his team nodded in numb agreement, Glenn Lazarus stood up and disagreed. Lazzo told coach Bennett he wanted people to be in awe of the team and to believe they were above the rest. As it turned out Lazarus's instinct was spot on because the Broncos' aura gave them an edge and it was every bit as important as the collective skills of their impressive players' roster.

None of my media matters have had quite the impact of my throwaway comments in the lead up to St George-Illawarra–Melbourne clash. It was the grand final replay and the hailstorm of abuse and criticism aimed at me following our 70–10 loss in round five of the 2000 season was incredible, to say the least. While my previous comments about having no sex before a game and Laurie Daley running on old legs had caused a mighty stir, nothing—and I mean nothing—had triggered such a response. It seemed everyone who was anyone (and then

some) wanted to have a piece of me. Unfortunately, the Dragons didn't only lose but were defeated by sixty humiliating
points, which gave many of my detractors in the media an
opportunity to kick my butt, big-time. However, what riles me
is that the actual interview was nowhere near as hardhitting or
as controversial as the pre-match publicity had made it out to
be. The interview was conducted by Adam Lucias (AL) of The
Media Game, a company contracted by the NRL to feed out
Rugby League stories to the television stations. What still amazes
me is that it was a 'nothing' interview, just a few throwaway
lines hyped to the enth degree by the media.

It didn't worry me at the time—still doesn't, to be honest—
because in my heart-of-hearts, I still believe we should have
been the last premiers of the 20th century.

Indeed, the 1999 Grand Final will long be seen by Dragons
fans as the one which got away because there are still a few
unanswered questions and controversial incidents which arose
from the game. For instance, I still can't understand why the
NRL changed referees mid-week. The Matt Geyer try will
always be clouded by controversy, while the penalty try
awarded to Craig Smith in the dying stages of the match could
have gone either way. So when I was asked by Lucias whether
Melbourne were 'worthy' premiers, I said no. However, what
was left out of the newspaper copy was that I thought Melbourne was still a dangerous unit and we had to be right on
our game.

In the wake of the loss the club placed a gag on me and the
rest of the team. As a result of all the drama, rumours started.
One printed in the *Daily Telegraph* claimed that an unnamed
team-mate (Craig Smith) tired of my antics and had whacked me
on the jaw. It was nothing more than a downright lie—and a
laughable one at that. I've included the entire transcript of the

'Melbourne aren't worthy winners' interview to prove it was nowhere near as bad as the press made it out to be. I'll leave it to you to judge.

**Adam Lucias:** Anthony, a grand final replay but neither side is travelling too well at the moment.

**AM:** No we're not. Both sides are really keen for a win, they haven't got one yet and this is their first game . . . it's going to be spectacular . . . at the MCG . . . we want to stay up there in contention for the top eight so it's an important one for us.

**AL:** A few encouraging signs from Saturday night?

**AM:** Yeah, the guys fought really well. I thought we deserved the two points but it didn't swing our way but everyone's got more confidence about them and we're ready to take the next step.

**AL:** What do you think of Melbourne's form—none out of four? Not too many defending premiers have come back from that?

**AM:** No. They're still a strong team all round the park. You can't underplay them at all; really have to be on our game. I see us as the champions and we're going down there to prove that to not just ourselves but everybody else.

**AL:** You've been quoted as saying you consider yourself champions. That last-second try must still hurt.

**AM:** Oh man, we know we had it, we know we blew it. That's why it's going to be a great game, great atmosphere. Hopefully the people can get there from down Melbourne and whoever's coming from Sydney and witness the grand final replay, hopefully in favour of the other side [us].

**AL:** There's still a bit of speculation about that last-minute try in the grand final. Have you had a chance to look at it over the off-season? Still go along with the ruling?

**AM:** No . . . there's still a lot of questions in the game; a forward pass to Matt Geyer; the last try . . . very controversial. There's a lot of points you can put out but can't undo it. We've got to go down there and prove to them and ourselves and especially our fans, you know, we should be the number one team.

**AL:** Do you still consider them worthy premiers given that it was a last-minute controversial try?

**AM:** I don't really feel they deserved to win but they got the win. But we're going to find out on Friday night. Be a good match, that's what everyone's looking forward to.

**AL:** Plenty of dangerous players in their side. Got to keep your eye on anyone in particular?

**AM:** I think they're good players. I feel they're most dangerous thing is their offloads . . . you know, (Steve) Kearney and (Rodney) Howe; there's Ross sniffing up around the rucks. That's probably the main danger.

**AL:** You clash on the MCG, it's a special arena isn't it?

**AM:** I haven't actually played there before but what they say is it's a great arena to play at—atmosphere great—and go down there and take it all in.

**AL:** How do you think the Melbourne people will support the game?

**AM:** They better get out there. Because if they don't they might be five zip.

Not much there, eh? Nevertheless, my quotes were plastered on the back page of the newspapers; they headlined the radio bulletins and chewed up so much prime time on the evening news you'd have sworn I insulted the Prime Minister! It got out of hand and the Storm supporters vented their anger at me whenever I touched the ball. Throughout the game they chanted

'Mundine's a wanker' and I would have done a little dance to their tune had we not been flogged 70–10!

The media, especially Ray Hadley at 2UE, and a group of old Dragons like Johnny Raper, Graeme Langlands and Craig Young, went to town. They said I gave Melbourne the inspiration and motivation to win the match by bagging them. Langlands said I was driving him away from the club . . . though I didn't make him become a talent scout for Sydney Roosters the previous year. Raper had his say, albeit cautiously after our previous run-in when I called him a 'yesterday's man'. Craig Young gave me a tough time. Ian Walsh said the club was scared of being branded racist if it took action against me.

For two weeks our co-captains Nathan Brown and Craig Smith, coach David Waite and chief executive Brian Johnston were the only people who could talk shop. On my arrival at Sydney Airport I was confronted by a throng of media and all I could say were short things such as, 'I'll be back, baby, just like Arnold Schwarzenegger.'

The criticism by old players annoyed me. Who are they? They're still getting drunk on nostalgia and free grog at the club, and they're loud and obnoxious and I've heard stories about what they've done away from the field and it's a lot worse than anything I've ever been guilty of. And, because of what I know, I treat their claims that I'm this and I'm that with a pinch of salt and a shrug of my shoulders. My ever-so-humble tip to them is to stop living in the 1970s, get out of the bar, and spend some quality time with their family.

In the wake of the sixty-point flogging to the Storm the *Sunday Telegraph* on 5 March pinpointed ten things which were wrong with the Dragons, citing such things as player morale, a lack of depth, coach David Waite, big heads, our defence and our attack. Yet, do you know who topped the list of problems?

Me. According to reporters Cameron Bell and Adam Hawse the biggest problem for St George-Illawarra was 'Anthony Mundine's pre-match hysteria.'

While plenty of people were struggling to find excuses to hide behind after our shut-out, I took a lot away from the experience. I learned there is plenty a man must learn and accept from such a defeat and I realised I couldn't avoid the fact I was outplayed on the night. The Storm's Scott Hill had a blinder. I realised I had to deal with the pressure of failure and it damn well hurt. But like Muhammad Ali I fell back on the belief that a man can be knocked to the ground but his spirit needn't go down with his body. The public also had their say and while there was plenty of support for me, many bayed for my blood. The *Daily Telegraph* published half a page of letters and they came from all over the place and they either hailed or crucified me. Here are some of them.

It pains and sickens me when I hear yobbos at the football and cricket calling anyone a wanker or any other derogatory names. I can sure appreciate Tony Mundine taking offence on behalf of his son. These yobbos wouldn't dare say it to his face. I took my own son especially to see Mundine play our great game just so when he grows old he will be able to say he saw The Man play, just as I went to see Bob Fulton.

I am neither a St George nor Manly supporter but can admire a great footballer when I see one.

Players like this should be cherished or respected to say the least.

GEOFF PEACOCK, LLANDILO

Surely 70 to 10 will button-up those loose lips of Anthony Mundine.

His boorish comments have become tiresome. If his tackling was in the same proportion to his racial sensitivities, then the difference in the scores would have been a lot lower.
LYLE KEATS, MIRANDA

I am writing in to say how sick and tired I am of hearing how Anthony Mundine should be dropped from the St George team because of the comments he made before last weekend's game. The reports are half right.

He should be dropped not because of what he said but because of his lack of ability on the field.

Time and again there is a smoke-screen put up about what he has said and nothing said about his performance on the field, but if he is the greatest as he likes everybody to believe I am watching the wrong game.

I thought to be a great player, especially the best five-eighth in the game, you had to not only be good with the ball in your hands but you also have to tackle. That's right, Anthony—tackle. That's where you get your red and white jersey a little dirty.

I would say this has a lot to do with your not getting picked in the rep teams. Maybe tackle is a racist word so Anthony wants nothing to do with it.

It's time to let this overrated player slide back to First Division where he belongs—that's if the St George-Illawarra selectors have the guts to make the decision against the almighty Anthony Mundine.
DARREN WOOD, FAIRY MEADOW

Less than twenty-four hours after Melbourne walloped us by a cricket score at the MCG the switchboard at Radio 2GB almost went into meltdown mode, with people phoning the likes of Jon

Harker and Johnny Gibbs to air their thoughts on The Man. They included 'Paul' who told the panel:

> Just on Anthony Mundine when he says those comments his tongue is set so firmly in his own cheek, he's laughing . . . it's different when you read it in the paper but I saw him make a comment where he said something along the lines that he should have been in the Australian team three years ago and to him the team was incomplete and he couldn't get the words out for laughing at his own comment.

John Gibbs, the former international, described my crucifixion as a smoke-screen for a club in crisis. Artie Beetson said I should take the 'John Wayne approach' and shut up. He reckoned I didn't have to provide the opposing team with any extra incentive. Mark Coyne said it was superficial for a lot of the finger pointing at St George-Illawarra to be directed my way. David Moffett, the head of the NRL, said he admired me because I speak my mind, adding Rugby League needed characters. Another caller, 'Grant', told the panel:

> I know you're probably sick of hearing about Mundine but just a bit in his defence. Has anyone sort of thought he's out there saying we're going to go down there to Melbourne and we're goin' to show 'em who the champions are . . . has anyone thought if maybe the rest of his team backed him and took the same attitude . . . that's what got him there in the first place.

The things I say are harmless, but I believe them. I don't set people up for personal ridicule. When I said Laurie Daley was running on old legs in 1997, I just meant that not only was there a young turk coming through, but he was determined to dethrone him. It was a challenge—and Daley took it in the right spirit. Some say it's just a kid with a chip on his shoulder talking it up. But I am also well aware that every time I say I'm the greatest—*every time*—it means a lot to young Aboriginal kids. I know from meeting them that such hype helps give them hope—a belief—and that's worth all the barbs and arrows that have so far been slung my way.

That night in Melbourne was a big wake-up call. Before that I had never included the team or my team-mates in my pre-match hype and it coincided with a humiliating defeat. But I realised, as I trudged off the MCG, it wasn't right to speak for the club because while I am able to live up to my comments, it was unfair to lay that on my team-mates. Nevertheless, I revelled in the idea that Raper, Langlands, Young and the old Saints players figured I was beaten and broken. They couldn't have been more wrong because every word of their criticism gave me the desire to get back and rub their noses in my success. I was so keen to get back on the paddock I could have burst. And what a lot of the media overlooked was that before I told a camera crew how I thought St George-Illawarra were the real champions, no-one expected the Storm–Dragons crowd to pass the 10,000 mark. Yet when The Man spoke almost 25,000 turned out in the Melbourne rain to call me a 'wanker'. Believe me, I took that as a mighty tribute and not an insult, and I believe many of those people will come out to watch me as a boxer.

To be brutally honest the Rugby League culture doesn't appeal to me in the slightest. It's macho and laced with false bravado. It isn't a scene for a free spirit because in Rugby League it's all right to be an individual as long as everyone else is the same. I say I am The Man and the League world goes into a frenzy, yet players create bad headlines and there's a thousand apologists falling over themselves to make excuses for them. A bunch of footballers go to the cricket, throw cups of urine on other patrons and bully kids, and it's described as letting off steam. Graham Richardson, the former senator and an avid St George supporter, used the example of a St George player who broke a woman's jaw on the Gold Coast in 1977 to highlight the capacity of some footballers to misbehave. I can't see myself doing something like that; it's not in my character.

While I'm a cleanskin, Rugby League is a repressed culture and whenever an individual—such as me—rattles the cage the older brigade in the game's hierarchy and media don't know how to handle it. They panic and think of ways to clamp down on him. When it comes to me I suspect what irks the older generation most of all is it's an Aboriginal kid doing all the talking. They grew up in an era when Aborigines weren't even citizens; they were seen as scum and I think that thought is instilled in many of these people. Indeed, I'm told of one former club official who made it known to his mates in the press he believed a team had a chance of winning a title with one Aborigine in the ranks, a lesser chance with two, and no hope with three. When you scan your eyes over his club's teams in the past then it seems as if he made sure there were never more than one or two brothers in his club. It worried some people to hear me give my thoughts on issues footballers aren't supposed to talk about—racism, religion, politics, injustice. I was seen as a black duck flying over a swamp and every time they had the chance the old boys tried to shoot me down. Indeed, in the wake of the MCG massacre, ex-international Ian Walsh made it clear he thought the club was 'too scared' to take any action against me for making comments to the press because of the supposed fear of being branded 'racist'. It was nonsense, but it gave an insight into the depth of feeling against me. The criticism of the Rapers and the Langlands didn't upset me, but it hurt those around me.

On many occasions I was asked whether it was worth the effort. But why should I have surrendered the right to express my views? For many in the game and, dare I suggest, political circles, my mouth is seen as a dangerous weapon and they're like nuclear protesters trying to shut me down. When St George gagged me after the Storm defeated us I abided by their orders because I didn't want to be seen as the person who destroyed the club at a vulnerable time in its history.

One group of people who have been forgotten by many in Rugby League are the loyal fans. As footballers have been elevated to superstar status, many have become aloof from the people who have helped them gain the big money and prestige. Everyone is entitled to their moods, but I don't think it's fair to follow the example of some blokes and avoid fans after a game. After last year's grand final loss I made a point of leaving the official function upstairs and passing through the security guards employed to keep the public at bay so I could spend time with our fans. I knew they wanted to share their pain after going through the highs and lows of an amazing season and, as it turned out, meeting with members of the Dragons' Army was great therapy for me. I don't restrict my keeping in touch with the average Joe to the footy ground, however. At the time of my writing this book, for instance, I'd submitted plans to Kogarah Council to open a boxing gymnasium for the area's youth. If it is given the green light, I and a few other athletes like Solomon and Nathan Blacklock will man the gym every day so we are on hand to offer advice on living the right kind of life. It's my intention to pass on the lessons my dad taught me.

I myself learned the importance of being humble and available to people when in 1995 I went to Sydney airport with *Rugby League Week* photographer John Elliott to try to get a cover shot with the US basketball hero Magic Johnson. Johnson's All-Stars had been in Australia to play the Boomers national squad and we decided to meet him on spec at Sydney Airport on his return to the Harbour City from Perth. Johnson's reaction made me feel pretty small. It was obvious he didn't want to do it. His manager gave it the go-ahead. I'd been a fan of Magic's. I'd watched in awe his efforts in the National Basketball Association. I'd cheered him and the Dream Team when they won the Olympic gold and, like the rest of the world, I was so very sorry for him when he contracted HIV. Yet, when I met him I wondered whether he was worth the effort. I'm still sorry for his bad luck. But as for the rest—thinking he was great, thinking he had something worth aspiring to—I lost a lot of respect for him that day on account of his impatient sighs and hostile body language. It taught me plenty; it taught me no matter how far I go in life I won't ever act like that when I meet someone.

One thing I do value in the Rugby League culture is the mateship creed. During my time in the big league I have made some very close pals, none more than Dragons hooker Nathan Brown. He's a great bloke who makes no excuses for a loss and does not gloat in victory. He sticks up for his players and he accepts the responsibilities of his job. Browny is one bloke I would gladly fight for and I know he feels the same about me.

While I know there'll be people snapping at my heels until the day I die because I'm different and not a company man, I take great heart in a quote from Albert Einstein, who said of those that dare to be different: 'Great spirits have always encountered violent opposition from mediocre minds.' Amen, Albert, baby, and your thoughts are never truer than in the brutal science of Rugby League.

# CHAPTER 14

# STATE OF PLAY

I may have turned my back on Rugby League, but I still think it is a good game and I hope one day the hierarchy allow it to fulfil its potential. I'm adamant boxing is *the* sport, but I still appreciate the skills and excitement of League. And it's not easy to make it to the Big League because a top grader needs plenty of God-given gifts including speed, turn of pace, balance, defensive skills, a lack of fear, and intuition, enterprise and a class which can't be taught at any school. The talent comes from within; it's God-given, brother, and I was lucky to have been smiled upon from high in that regard, although I do concede other people have their gifts and I respect them.

So while I have rejected it as the sport for me, I believe Rugby League is a great game for children. It teaches them the value of teamwork—it's great to see kids unite and work together as a unit—and it promotes good health and fitness. If the coach and manager are decent people they can help raise a player's sense of self-esteem too, thus assisting in taking a kid from the mean streets to respectability.

I am grateful to Rugby League for giving me so many opportunities, but I am dirty the politics did not allow me to fulfil my potential. It's incredible to think my being able to run with the ball has allowed me to use my voice to scream out about the injustices against the Aboriginal people and other social issues. Rugby League has also allowed me to befriend some great individuals from all walks of life. Since being graded with the

Dragons I've met people down on their luck and I've dined with people who are extremely wealthy and powerful, but I haven't allowed it to change me as a person.

The early part of the 21st century offers Rugby League plenty of stiff competition from such sports as Aussie Rules and international Rugby Union. If the people running Rugby League aren't wary they'll lose even more ground in a limited market. They have to realise it is first and foremost entertainment, and the hierarchy has to start making players realise that in this age of multimedia they're not just mere footballers anymore. They're entertainers and people have to be able to relate to them and want to cheer them. Mark my words, Rugby League won't grow without its characters, but the hierarchy has to raise them up and encourage them—not stamp on them like they are bugs. I also believe we have to do more to entice kids from multicultural backgrounds to embrace Rugby League as their game because there's a lot of untapped talent out there begging for a chance.

At the time of my writing this book there is constant debate about the modern game with both old players and fans complaining about such rules as the interchange and the ten metres. But what I like about the game is it's now fast paced, it's explosive, it's full throttle and the fans have to concentrate to keep up with it. You don't blink at some games for fear of missing something. My fear is some coaches deny their players the chance to truly play their own natural game because they're too scared to try something that might result in a cross being put next to their name. The pressure not to drop a ball or miss a tackle is intense and I know it's taken the enjoyment away from some players.

While I know some people will hate them, these are my thoughts on some of the more contentious issues in the game:

## The unlimited interchange bench

*The critics say:* Opponents of the interchange bench claim it has taken a lot of the gladiatorial content out of the game and that it actually increases the chance of injuries because the backs are pitted against 110 kilo forwards who are being rotated in ten minute bursts while the halfback and centres and wingers and pivot don't have a break. Others say it has led to the increased emphasis on tries being scored from kicks because it's too hard to break a 'rested' defensive line. At the time of this book going to press there was a concerted move to scrap it.

*The Man says:* I'm adamant the unlimited interchange is great for the game. It helps make Rugby League explosive, fast and dynamic. The idea that a player can come back to the field feeling fresher helps a fast game retain its momentum and that can only be a good thing.

## The mid-air rule

*The critics say:* My former co-coach Andrew Farrar is one who does not like the mid-air rule because he thinks it can't be penalised. Others say the joke of the rule is it is only applied to kicks and not to such incidents as a player taking a high pass—like the time Cronulla's David Peachey landed on his head after being tackled mid-air when he jumped to take a high pass against the Northern Eagles.

*The Man says:* Any rule aimed at protecting the player has to be seen as a good one and needs to be given a fair go. When a player is airborne he is defenceless and it scares me to think of what could happen if a player was clipped while he was in the air and landed square on his head. The results could be fatal. I think they should extend the rule to embrace both kicks and passes.

**The dead-ball line rule**

*The critics say:* This is the rule which allows a player to 'kill' a good in-goal kick by placing a foot over the dead-ball line and then collecting the rolling ball so his team gains a twenty-metre restart. Many people believe it doesn't reward good kicks and it's a 'soft' option.

*The Man says:* It has created plenty of drama but the rules are there for everyone to use. While this rule has been in place for years, it might be time to look at scrapping it.

**Quick play-the-ball and the ten-metre rule**

*The critics say:* The ten-metre rule and play-the-ball is leading to a one-dimensional game. It means the defensive team is constantly on the back foot and the attacking team, especially the dummy half, makes easy ground. Nippy halfbacks and powerful frontrowers make up to fifteen metres a go for five tackles. The game is fast becoming more like touch football.

*The Man says:* If you revert to the old five-metre rule it will become a game of attrition and close the attack right down. At the moment the game is geared towards excitement, and the people in the stands and outer ground are getting a good mix of free-flowing football and crunching defence.

# CONTROVERSY

# CHAPTER 15

# MEDIA MADNESS

*Anthony Mundine . . . just announced he was barring himself from sex before matches. Actually, in Anthony's case maybe that should read he has barred women from having sex with him before matches.*

The Sunday Telegraph, *Mike Colman*

The media by definition is meant to be objective—display no bias, report the facts and deliver both sides of the story. In my dealings with the Rugby League press, I've come to the conclusion that some journalists need to be reminded of their responsibilities because they either aren't aware of them or they choose to totally ignore them. I don't think a great many consider the ramifications of their throwaway lines and bold headlines—they're things which can bring an individual's family to tears.

There are some good guys in the fourth estate, including Danny Wiedler, Ray Warren and Ian Heads. But a few of the others, especially the older brigade, leave me feeling Arctic cold. The way I've scoped the Rugby League media scene is that they seem to handpick their favourites and champion their causes at *every* possible opportunity. Me? I'm like Othello from the Shakespeare play, brother, because I'm black; I speak the truth and give insights which really aren't appreciated—but don't worry, Chocy baby isn't going to end up a Shakespearian tragedy because I'm going to thrive. However, what hurts me when I see another of 'their' boys having his barrow pushed is knowing the public actually reads it and, worse still, many believe it! It sickens me.

It galls me when I read about and hear some reporters and commentators carry on about me because I have no time for them. What have they done? I'm not saying a person has to be a former footballer to cover the game, because most of those guys are just as bad as the others. But I ask, what have the people in the media done for humanity? The way they talk and write about me they sound as if they're my superiors. But on what grounds? What causes have they stood up for? Have they ever put everything on the line for their beliefs? The reason I was unpopular with some was because I said what I believed to be true—have the members of the press who criticise me ever taken such a stand? While they might not upset me with their poison pens and barbed tongues, they do have the capacity to hurt my family and the people close to me. But they hide behind their positions and are a bunch of slaves who have to answer to their editors. Sometimes I think of their lot and I pity them.

When I first arrived on the scene I was seen as a quiet, multi-skilled kid. The media were well aware I had the choice of competing at the highest level in three sports. Yet the way they wrote about me was as if I was only playing for St George because of my family name. Every story mentioned I was the son of boxing great Tony Mundine. The more I read it, the more it sounded as if I wasn't there on my own merits, and as much as I love and admire my dad, I didn't like it at all. I waited and, after I found my feet in the big league and bared my teeth with the Dragons and Brisbane, they started to call me 'arguably the best' when I *was* the best. It offended me, because not only did the media underplay my performances but they confirmed they're scared to crown a new kid for fear of putting their own boys' noses out of joint. They've had numerous opportunities to acknowledge me because I never walked off the field second to Laurie Daley and Brad Fittler. But I get the impression most journalists would prefer to swallow poison than say that.

Actually, I'm proud of my record against the likes of Daley and Fittler, who had a posse of big match winners playing alongside them. I was forced to do a lot of mine off my own back because during my time at St George we had, at best, two match winners. When I returned to Kogarah from Brisbane I helped transform the Dragons from cellar dwellers to red-hot contenders for the title. Yet no-one flipped out over my efforts. There was no call from the press for Mundine to play for the Test side or to make the origin team. Instead there was a deafening silence. There was, however, an abundance of resentment from journalists who didn't appreciate my comments and proclamations, even though my words helped make their jobs easier! But I think that says more about them than it does me.

When I told the *Sun Herald*'s Danny Wiedler about banning myself from sex before a game because it drained me of energy, it led to a veritable firestorm of abuse from the press. Maybe it was envy, man, envy that a young brother from the mean streets was in *that* kind of demand. But some of their comments became very personal, and their snide remarks upset my mum, dad and other members of my family. That's where it hurts, when they upset those close to you. When I got home after the 2UE switchboard had run red hot with calls bagging me, Dad, Mum and Uncle Mick were waiting. They were in tears for me. Their hearts had been broken by the terrible things they'd heard on the radio. With tears in his dark, proud eyes Dad told me I couldn't leave myself open to such criticism like that ever again. He and Uncle Mick said I had to keep my mouth shut. But I told them not to worry because all my critics were doing was fuelling my desire; they'd given me another reason to make them eat their words. However, my family's tearful reaction to the criticism taught me that while the media mightn't have the power or capacity to get to me, they can hurt people I love and I damn them for that.

Nevertheless, I have had some good supporters, including 2UE's Alan Jones, and Ray Warren, the voice of Rugby League on Channel Nine. When the St George legends lined up to kick me up the backside after the MCG massacre early in the 2000 season, Alan Jones took a stand and sang my virtues. I don't think he knows how much I appreciated the boost and support. Warren is the only one who has put everything on the line to call me a superstar, and I appreciate the courage of his convictions. Ray once told Dad that two words could solve all my media problems: 'No comment'. I appreciate Ray's concern; he's a good man. But why should I be gagged?

In April 1998, a week after my 'sex ban', the *Sunday Telegraph* launched a literary assault on me. Among the writer's graffiti were such gems as saying that I could take my place among the great Aborigine athletes, or be remembered as a blowhard. The paper said I could be the most exciting player in the game or a dud. 'Like the sex ban, the choice is his. Anthony Mundine has the opportunity to be important. Or impotent.'

One thing I can assure you is I'm not impotent. While some journalists say I'm all mouth and little action, they should have opened their eyes and watched the game more closely. With the advent of cable television we have seen a glut of former stars assume the role of commentators. And while there are plenty of people who call the likes of Wally Lewis and Brett Kenny 'experts' I find they are too bogged down in their own bias to give praise to those who deserve it. They may have been outstanding, unconventional players in their day but they certainly run with the flow when it comes to picking players.

At the same time, the media is open to manipulation. I do it by making my bold statements. If I want to highlight the Aboriginal cause I only have to ring a few reporters and they'll jump. They'll sniff a headline, and be my best friend for a few minutes and they'll push everything, from me wanting to run for politics to my trumpeting myself as the best five-eighth in the world. Other players get what they want by being the nice guy and putting on a smile when they'd actually like to throttle the reporter. But what really makes me grin is knowing my detractors in the media—no matter how much they may loathe me and all I stand for—will drop *everything* to put their byline on a story featuring me. And that leads me to ask what kind of creature that makes them.

**Postscript**

After I came out and made comments about the state of play and the state of the world, the *Sunday Telegraph* did a poll of prominent senior players in 1996 and asked for their honest thoughts on my antics. I have to admit some of their reactions— their overwhelming support—brought surprise to my big brown eyes.

*Laurie Daley:* He's a good young talent and I haven't got a problem with him. The way he speaks out is not my go but it's a free world and he can do what he likes.

*Paul Langmack:* Anthony's a great player and he obviously has a lot of confidence. He's a lovely bloke—but he's in the wrong country. If he was living in America his antics would be accepted but in Australia he cops a bagging. Everyone's different but I don't know why you would put added pressure on yourself. It's not my concern how he carries on, but good luck to him.

*Glenn Lazarus:* Everyone's got the right to say what they want. I think it's a shame not everyone says what they feel. Some players are perhaps too pedestrian and don't often give their own thoughts. I think with Anthony, the media finds him new and fresh and that's why they jump over everything he says.

*Jason Taylor:* I think players do their talking on the field, but in saying that, I think it's definitely another avenue for promoting the game. Some players can be a bit the other way and not say enough. Perhaps we need a few more characters in the game because people like that—but then you can take things too far.

*Tony Butterfield:* If you believe in making your goals public, then go for your life. It's not my cup of tea—it would look ridiculous coming from my mouth. He's putting pressure on himself, but maybe he enjoys that pressure.

*Mark Soden:* I think he's got to start worrying about his own performances rather than having his name in lights. If he's as good as he says he is all that will come to him. He's taken the American approach of blowing his own trumpet and the fans won't cop it. In Australia, the people love knocking the tall poppy off and that's what's happening to him.

*Sean Garlick:* It's a little un-Australian. Australians don't like hearing people say how good they are—they admire the humble approach. It's nothing against him, but I wouldn't be doing it.

# CHAPTER 16

# OLD LEGS, NEW SPUNK

*Laurie Daley is running on old legs. I'm fresh. I've got young legs. It's time for the new generation, brother. It's time for us to have a go.*
*My most famous challenge, 1997*

L aurie Daley was in camp on the New South Wales south coast with the state's Tri-series team when he read my most celebrated challenge—and I'm told he didn't miss a beat. While his team-mates tried to get an angry reaction from him by pointing out the headlines I generated by screaming for the selectors to give me a shot at him, the Canberra skipper from all reports refused to buy into it. Apparently Daley just smiled to himself, shrugged his shoulders and kept eating his breakfast.

My challenge was ridiculed by an army of people, but I like to think Daley, at least, took it seriously because I wanted him to. That 'old legs' statement was the first of many steps to establish myself as 'The Man'. I trumpeted myself as the man born to be king, and I didn't care who knew about it. I was sick of saying what people wanted to hear; I felt caged like a tiger in the zoo. I wanted to emancipate my voice box, I wanted to be free and honest, I didn't want to be fake. I backed myself against Laurie when I made that statement because as much as I admired him as a great player and a humble man—and I still do—I'd finished with a points decision against him on our two previous outings. And, just for the record, in our subsequent meetings since 1997 I haven't lost to him—or to Fittler, for that matter.

There are plenty of good five-eighths around, including Matthew Johns and Kevin Walters—but I know I have skills they don't possess. Last year I was walking down the street and this old man said, 'Hey, Mundine.' Because I'm polite I turned around and said, 'How are you, sir?' He asked whether I really was the Anthony Mundine he watched play for the Dragons every weekend. When I confirmed this, the man told me he was sixty-two, had followed the Dragons for as long as he could remember and had cheered them on during their eleven straight titles. He'd seen Raper, Provan, Gasnier, Langlands and Walsh play, but he paid me the ultimate compliment by saying he'd witnessed me do things that no other player would even dare dream of. I was moved, man. And I looked him square in the eye and said, 'I'm going to keep it up, sir.'

So, even while I appreciated Laurie's reaction of taking it on the chin, I was still desperate to try to upstage Daley for the Super League Australian jumper. I not only considered declaring myself a Queenslander in an attempt to get an opportunity to oppose him in a high-level showdown, but I wanted people to hear I was far from intimidated by the man who was then ranked alongside his Raiders team-mate Bradley Clyde as the world's best player. My first step was to talk to the *Sun Herald* and my words were like blisters.

> Speaking like a prize fighter before he enters the ring, Mundine has hit Daley with a surprise left by virtually declaring the Australian captain is past his prime and [saying] he is hoping to floor him sooner than later. 'Laurie Daley is running on old legs. I'm fresh. I've got young legs. It's time for the new

generation, brother. It's time for us to have a go. I want to be
up against Laurie Daley as soon as possible.'

So I was sweating on crossing swords with him. Even though I
still desperately needed to boost my fitness after an injury, my
confidence was so high I figured I could still outplay him.
People say such behaviour is that of an attention-seeker, and I
won't disagree because at that stage I was chasing publicity with
a capital 'P'. You see, even way back in 1997 when I was only
twenty-one, I realised the national selectors had their boys, and
before he retired from representative football in 1999 Laurie was
definitely one of them. Good luck to him: I'm not bitter. Actually, it was an honour to have played alongside him in his last
State of Origin campaign in 1999. I'm not kidding when I say I
was mightily impressed by the ovation Daley, Cronulla's
Andrew Ettingshausen and Newcastle enforcer Paul Harragon
received when they did a lap of honour around the running
track of the brand-new Stadium Australia. As people stayed
back in their thousands after the game to cheer the trio I was
happy to learn that Daley harboured no resentment about my
'old legs' comment.

In fact, at my father's insistence, I had phoned Laurie in the
wake of all this to clear the air. I have to admit it was hard for
me to talk to him, but the conversation went something like this:

Laurie: 'Well, why did you say it?'
Mundine: 'Because I want to play rep footy.'
Laurie: 'Yeah, well, fair enough, mate.'

One thing which does impress me about Daley is that he is a
man of the people. I've been given examples of his compassion,
like the time he did a photo shoot for *Rugby League Week* by

the banks of a river in Queanbeyan. An old Aboriginal man, down on his luck and sleeping in the bushes, lurched out from his shelter and upon recognising Daley wanted to hug him. Daley didn't blink. The old bloke got his hug—and some kind words. I've heard similar tales which paint a picture of a decent man.

# CHAPTER 17

# GREEN AND GOLD NIGHTMARE

*They [the selectors] have their boys and obviously we aren't part of their future.*

*On missing out on the 1999 Australian team*

I finally realised I had gone as far as an outspoken Aborigine could possibly go in Rugby League when the selectors over-looked me for the Australian Tri-series team which played Great Britain and New Zealand at the end of the 1999 season. Look at the tapes from that season and then ask who was the game's best pivot? Being overlooked was *the* greatest disappointment I've experienced as a professional athlete and the emptiness I felt after the team was announced even outweighed the heartache of watching Melbourne steal the premiership title from under our nose—and brother, that was dark.

After the names were read past 'M' they all seemed to melt into one another: Darren Britt, Brad Fittler, Bryan Fletcher, Matthew Gidley, Craig Gower, Rodney Howe, Matthew Johns, Brett Kimmorley, Nik Kosef, Darren Lockyer, Russell Richardson, Mat Rogers, Robbie Ross, Wendall Sailor, Darren Smith, Jason Smith, Gorden Tallis, Brad Thorn, Shaun Timmins, and Shane Webke. Where was Mundine? It stung—*really* stung—because I thought I'd done more than enough throughout the season to secure the green and gold jumper.

While we Dragons were extremely happy for Shaun Timmins for gaining his international spurs, I'm certain in their heart-of-hearts a few of the boys were upset the selectors overlooked me. Prior to the team's announcement it was widely tipped a few of us would make the test team, despite losing the grand final. That year—1999—was my big chance to fulfil the dream that had spurred me on as a youngster competing in the tough South Sydney competition. I'd finally broken into the New South Wales State of Origin squad and people started to realise what I'd always told them—I had plenty to offer. When I missed out on the Tri-series team I concluded I was hoping against all hope of ever making the national side and my heart dropped like a stone. I lost it big time and my fury was also fuelled by the omission of Cronulla Sharks fullback David Peachey, one of the NRL's most electrifying players, as well as my Dragons team-mate Nathan Blacklock, who finished the '99 season acknowledged by even the harshest critics as the code's most dangerous winger. In my mind there was a set against us, and after my previous fallouts with one of the selectors—Johnny Raper—I went into overdrive.

While I concede my grand final performance was a long shot from my best effort—it should be remembered I was on a drip for four days fighting tonsillitis—the longer I spent trying to work out why we three were overlooked by the ARL selectors the more it seemed we missed the cut because we were Aborigines. My views, aired on Channel Ten's *Sports Tonight* program, created a hailstorm of controversy, and as soon as those words left my mouth there was a long line of people wanting to shoot me down.

The transcript of the interview with *Sports Tonight* reporter Peter Ryan reads like this:

**PR:** I have with me a surprise omission from the Australian team, Anthony Mundine. Anthony, what was your reaction when you found you weren't in the squad?

**AM:** You guys wouldn't be here interviewing me if you didn't think it was an injustice. The way I feel is Chris Anderson and the selectors have their bunch and they dictate what goes on and who is in the team and who's not. Call it a dictatorship if you want. I don't feel that it's the form team or the best team on the paddock, you know, they have their boys. Like, for instance, Nathan Blacklock scored twenty four tries this year, led the scoring in the finals series, the Dally M winger of the year. He wasn't chosen. Another one, David Peachey he's been the most potent winger this season. He stands out . . . above everyone, I feel . . . and he wasn't chosen, and myself. And we're all Aboriginal and we're all proud.

**PR:** You think you haven't been selected because of the colour of your skin?

**AM:** Well, you can put one and one together. I'm sure you can . . . you're not silly.

**PR:** Mate, that's a pretty big call against the selectors.

**AM:** Well, like I said, they have their boys and we obviously aren't a part of their future. So, hey! I'm happy; I'm proud and I'm going about my business.

**PR:** Anthony Mundine speaking his mind as usual and no doubt we'll hear a lot more about this issue.

It didn't take long for me to hear the ARL's response, with national coach Chris Anderson and ARL boss Colin Love refuting my claims. The majority of my detractors said I was being stupid, and cited the selections of Gorden Tallis and Wendall Sailor to highlight my supposed ignorance. Others mentioned that one of the Test selectors, Arthur Beetson, was an Aborigine from Roma in the Queensland outback. The chairman of selectors, Eddie Lumsden, said my comments were stupid and I should shut my mouth in future because every time I said something I was jeopardising my chances of ever making the Australian side:

> When is this young man ever going to learn, when will he get the right advice? What he said was stupid. It's a bit of an insult, a slap in the face to one of the selectors, Arthur Beetson, who is an Aboriginal himself. It was a lot of nonsense. The side was picked on merit and form—it is ridiculous to suggest players missed out because of their backgrounds. Gorden Tallis and Wendall Sailor were chosen and they have Aboriginal back-grounds, so what is he talking about? We consider we came up with a very balanced side, full of form players and with a view towards next year's World Cup. Anthony Mundine isn't giving himself any chances of selection down the track.

I knew I'd be bucketed for my thoughts, but one person who hurt me by seeming to go out of his way to have a dig was my good mate Gorden Tallis. He basically told the press I was shooting my mouth off and what really upset me was he didn't have to buy into the argument at all. He could have kept a respectful silence but he didn't. He not only made it personal, but he went against me and I was consumed by a terrible sense of betrayal. Our friendship was so strong, one of the reasons I moved to Brisbane was to play football alongside him. Relations between us were strained, to say the least, and it wasn't until we met up at Nathan Brown's wedding before the kick-off of the 2000 season that we sat down, spoke and worked things out. I'm glad we did because the frost I felt has certainly thawed.

Wendall also disappointed me. When we played alongside one another with the Broncos in 1996 we were like brothers, and did things like play backyard cricket against one another on a daily basis. But when the bombs went off and they were exploding around me, Wendall didn't only go ducking for cover but said a few things about me to mutual friends he shouldn't have—things about my credibility—though we have spoken warmly since then.

A few other people used the example of the 1994 Kangaroo squad to further diminish my stance. They said the team was captained by Mal Meninga, who has Solomon Islander blood in him; vice-captain Laurie Daley had a full-blooded Aboriginal grandmother; Jim Serdaris is of Greek descent; Steve Renouf is Aboriginal; and so on. However, I countered that by saying they were the selectors' shiny-eyed boys who are pushed to the top at the expense of others because they say the right things, give no insight into their emotions, talk in clichés and go against their own beliefs to toe the line and keep their jumper. I'm different. I wouldn't change. Indeed, when I was a kid I made being picked for the Australian Rugby League team a major priority. I didn't realise then the crawling and sucking up that went with it. I always thought people were equal on the football field, but I was dead wrong.

Nathan Brown, who I think has been harshly dealt with by the rep selectors over the years, tried to douse the bushfire by telling the press he too thought I was off the mark in blaming my omission on race relations, although he agreed there was reason to believe my name had been scribbled in the selectors' black-banned book.

I think the selectors have a set against Choc. He's had a run in with them before and really I think a lot of people have a set against him because of his outspoken ways. I certainly couldn't understand his omission from the side and that's not taking anything away from Matthew Johns, who is a very good player and a good bloke. The suggestion that Johns was preferred because of his utility value is very hard to swallow. Anthony can cover a whole range of positions and apart from Brad Fittler, he was the best five-eighth and one of the very best players in the NRL this year. I just think the general public have a problem with Choc and the same goes with the selectors. David Peachey and Nathan Blacklock were also extremely unlucky to miss out as well.

Chris Anderson, the coach of the 1999 Australian team, explained that his side was picked on merit, telling the *Telegraph*'s Jon Geddes of my omission, 'They are tough decisions, there was nothing in it. Mundine is a great player, I have a lot of time for him, but you can't pick everyone.' Anderson also said I didn't miss the cut because of my grand final performance, saying no-one is picked or punted because of just one game. That comment only added further weight to my argument for selection because when you break down the statistics for the 1999 season I had it all over the national captain Brad Fittler. When he was complaining about an itch he couldn't scratch during the winter, the doctors diagnosed it as a rash called Mundine! Indeed, I & T Statistics, who compiled the match stats for Fox throughout the 1999 season, dissected Fittler's and my personal stats for the season and they read like this:

| ANTHONY MUNDINE | v | BRAD FITTLER |
|---|---|---|
| 23 | Games | 21 |
| 17 | Tries | 11 |
| 28 | Linebreaks | 20 |
| 4.22 | Kicks in play per game | 11.86 |
| 1.17 | Missed tackles per game | 1.33 |
| 14 | Try assists | 19 |

| 84 | Metres gained per game | 75 |
| 242 | Runs at the opposition line | 200 |

I know statistics don't always tell the full story, but the above suggests I had a good case for national selection. And while I maintain I was the world's best five-eighth, I also offered versatility because of my ability to be able to play fullback, wing, centre, five-eighth and hooker. I & T Statistics supported my claim on the eve of our Sydney Football Stadium semi-final clash that I had no reason to feel intimidated by the Roosters' skipper. And when I answered the *Daily Telegraph*'s Dean Ritchie's question as to whether I considered Fittler the game's finest pivot the headlines screamed: 'ANTHONY MUNDINE BLOWS HIS TRUMPET AGAIN!'

I don't know what they expected me to say. My reply to the reporter's question on Fittler was that everyone knew how I felt and, as The Man, I had no intentions of going back on my word. I was also asked by Ritchie whether I still considered myself the number one five-eighth:

I'm not intimidated [by Fittler] and I don't worry about the name of the player I'm playing. I won't get overawed. I'll just go out and do my job. Freddie is a great player and we always bring out the best in each other. I enjoy the challenge. I'm always ready to play. That's the way it has to be.

A further sidelight to the great stats facts was that Peachey was ahead of Robbie Ross in the fullback stakes with ten try assists (compared to Ross's two) while Nathan not only led the premiership's individual try-scoring tally, but he also broke the line forty times in twenty-six games! Make no mistake about it— we three bros were ripped off big time.

History shows national team selections have always been full of political intrigue. In 1948, the late Len Smith was alleged to have been left out of the Kangaroos' touring squad on religious grounds despite his being the Australian team's skipper against New Zealand earlier that year. Smith was a Catholic when the game was run by the Masons. Bobby McCarthy was left out of the 1973 Kangaroos despite being the game's most blockbusting forward. Benny Elias was overlooked for the 1996 tour because he was retiring, despite being acknowledged as the competition's best performed hooker. And the list goes on.

I think the time has finally come when the public—and the players—are told how the team is decided. As far as I'm concerned the only time the Australian team has been picked purely on form in recent times was during Super League. The likes of Solomon, David Peachey, Brad Thorn, Ken Nagas, Luke Priddis, Paul Green, Jason Stevens, Matt Adamson and Ryan Girdler were given their national jumpers against the Kiwis, French and English because the Super League hierarchy vowed the only criteria which would be taken into consideration when the team was selected was form, and with a capital 'F'. Unfortunately, I think the ARL places too heavy an emphasis on past performers and by doing so they're suffocating the dreams and hopes of a generation of players. What pushed me was knowing I was good enough to make the Australian team. Wearing that jumper was more than a dream—it was a mission. But the time came when I realised I was bashing my head against a brick wall. However, if the ARL was genuine in picking the side which best reflects true form they'd copy the American basketball system; the public votes for the NBA All Stars, and it's a proven way to reward the true performers in the world's elite basketball competition. I won't hold my breath for that to be implemented in this country because such a policy would have opened the door for a few 'bad' boys like A. Mundine to enter the inner sanctum.

While the Australians won the Tri-series tournament, I was picked for an Australian team—the AIRLAC Australian Aboriginal team—which played the Papua New Guinea Test team in Cairns and Campbelltown. I was thrilled to be considered but I respectfully declined the honour for three reasons. First, I was emotionally worn out. Second, the Aboriginal team was already good enough to beat the Kumuls. Third, my stepping aside allowed my cousin Blaine Stanley, who plays for the Sharks, the opportunity to play five-eighth in an international—and he slayed them. However, I had intended to be involved in the team because I believe it is the stepping stone for great things for Aboriginal footballers.

Indeed, I really regret we weren't to be represented in this year's World Cup in England, like the Maoris, because I reckon we could have rustled together a team which could have been a serious contender for the title. It would have been as follows: coach—Arthur Beetson; fullback—David Peachey; wing— Nathan Blacklock; centre—Ken McGuiness; centre—Laurie Daley; winger—Ken Nagas; five-eighth—Anthony Mundine; halfback—John Simon; lock—Cliff Lyons; second-row—Gorden Tallis; second-row—Wendall Sailor; prop—John Buttigeig; hooker—Dennis Moran; prop—Mark Tookey; reserves—Rod Silva, Albert Torrens, Justin Doyle, Lee Hookey, Sid Domic, Blaine Stanley, Robbie Simpson, Wes Patten, Owen Craigie. And yes, brother, it would be picked on form.

I know some people will say picking an Australian Aboriginal team is racist, but as I've already said I think it creates more opportunity for footballers who wouldn't otherwise get a sniff of rep football. The Maoris as a team have long been an institution in New Zealand and their existence hasn't caused any problems in their homeland. Indeed, to be a New Zealand Maori is a great honour and it would be great to think an Australian Aboriginal team could evoke the same emotion and pride in both our people and the entire nation. Arthur Beetson is keen for the Aborigines to be represented at the next World Cup and he's confident that at full strength they'd be title contenders. At worst, he says they could finish third; at best they'd be playing the Kangaroos in the final—and what a game that would be!

However, Arthur hit the nail on the head when he said the success of an Aboriginal representative team would depend upon the NRL clubs doing the right thing and giving players permission to play. As this book was being published the Australian Indigenous Rugby League Association was negotiating for a full-strength Aboriginal team to tour Great Britain for a five match tour in December.

While I found it satisfying to be considered a world class player, I knew it would be quite an empty feeling to be considered in the same breath as another St George Aborigine, Ricky Walford. Ricky ruled the flanks in his heyday but if you ask me, he too had a big problem in his game—and it had nothing to do with his defensive and attacking capabilities. I at least have an Australian Schoolboy's jumper and a Junior Kangaroos jumper in my top drawer at home. The beauty of them is that I was picked solely on form to wear them—and *no-one* can take that from me.

CHAPTER 18

# MY BLACKEST DAY

*We are setting a new standard. This kind of discrimination has been going on for 200 years and it's got to stop. Hopefully now my other brothers won't be afraid to speak out.*

*My thoughts after the NRL fined Barry Ward $10,000 for calling me a 'black c\*\*\*' in the 1998 semi-final elimination*

'm told by those who know Barry Ward that he's a decent, hardworking man from Sydney's south-western suburbs. They say he's very loyal and stands by his mates when the going gets tough. Unfortunately, I don't know that side of him. I'd like to, man, I would, but my only dealings with the chunky Bulldogs' forward have been in a verbal brawl about his sneering **'F\*\*\* you, you black c\*\*\*'** after a tackle during our bitterly fought elimination final loss to the Dogs in 1998.

I was shocked; the comment was like a sharp slap across my cheeks and it stopped me dead in my tracks. I hadn't heard the slur 'black c\*\*\*' since the dim, dark days of the juniors and God knows it hurt. Rather than cool down after the game, my blood boiled, and even now there are times when I think of the incident and I can't help but feel that I should have struck out at him. I know violence is wrong, but the jungle's law says if you want to mess with the lion then you risk being eaten.

When I was all alone after the match my reaction to the anger and frustration pent up inside of me wasn't to kick the crap out of a garbage bin or to scream in anger.

Instead I sat down and shed a stream of tears. I was *that* frustrated and the reason I cried over those two stupid words was because they made me feel my achievements as a footballer and a human being were insignificant—I was always going to be seen by some people as just another black c\*\*\*. People have since told me they were only words and that such sledging is just a part of football, but that's shallow. When you pick on someone because of the colour of their skin, then you are attacking their very being. Ward might not have realised the emotion his words would evoke in me when he uttered them, but they represented hatred and they cut me to the bone.

I didn't want to take the slur lying down; I wanted action. Despite protests from some friends who warned I'd be 'fried' by the game's hierarchy if I took the matter to the public arena, I phoned the *Sun Herald*'s Danny Wiedler and spilt my guts. I was agitated and infuriated and my tirade against the Bulldogs' player started a bonfire of claim and counter-claim.

When he was publicly named Ward said he didn't address the comment at me, insisting his words were instead directed at another St George player of Aboriginal descent, and my good friend, Robbie Simpson. Which doesn't make it any better. Ward accused Robbie of calling him a 'big fat c\*\*\*' and said he simply retaliated. The NRL tried to hose the drama down but I warned the matter would be taken to even higher channels, including the Human Rights Commission, if they didn't act on my complaint. They instigated a 'conciliation' meeting between Ward and me but, as I told the *Sydney Morning Herald*'s Steve Mascord the night before the encounter, a simple sorry was never going to be enough. 'If I had my way I wouldn't be there tomorrow,' I fumed. 'It's going to be pretty hard being in the same room as him. This is a very, very serious matter and I'll accept an apology after he's been seriously punished.'

The way I viewed the entire matter was *I* had complete control because I was the person who'd been wronged. What had really annoyed me in the lead up to the meeting, and then the subsequent investigation by the NRL board, was the constant cry that what is said on the field should be left there. No way. The people, including some media outlets, who demanded that should be ashamed of themselves. I was fighting to highlight wrongful behaviour. I was standing up for the Aboriginal kid who is spat at in the playground and the black girl who is called 'bitch' for no other reason than the pigmentation of her skin. It was groundbreaking and there were forces who wanted to sweep the drama aside, but I wouldn't budge. They said I was a troublemaker, involved in something I not only had no right to be involved in, but that I didn't understand. How dare they! I label that type of thinking barbaric; we don't live in the Dark Ages and no-one should be victimised physically or verbally on account of the colour of their skin or the name of their god. Do the same people believe violations which occur on the paddock, such as head-high tackles or elbows, should be left there? I dare say they don't. But what these people don't realise is being called a 'black dog'—*and worse*—is just as hurtful as any blow.

An interesting sidelight to the racial row came last year when I met Shannon Sharp, an African-American who plays for the Denver Broncos. He was genuinely shocked to hear of the incident and said had any white man uttered such a comment on an American football field there's no way he'd have been able to walk off—that's how sensitive an issue racist remarks are in the United States.

At the height of the drama it appeared as if everyone wanted me to let the incident go so I appreciated St George chief executive Brian Johnston respecting my decision to take the issue all the way. Solomon, who'd had an unhappy stint at Belmore, came out and offered his sign of solidarity by telling the press he believed the Canterbury-Bankstown club was a racist organisation. Solomon went as far as to say ethnic kids weren't given a fair chance to make the top grade. The club, and many of its supporters, tried to shoot Solomon down by saying the Bulldogs not only worked overtime to entice the many cultures who live in the Canterbury-Bankstown area to support their team, but that they also had a number of ethnic representatives in the first grade squad, including Lebanese-born Hazem El Masri, Samoan Willie Talau, Maori John Timu and Fiji's James Pickering, and the greatest trophy of all in the race row, Rod Silva, an Aboriginal fullback. Predictably enough, those same people said the comment which had offended me was nothing but a throwaway line. My opinion is their thoughts only served to highlight that such racist insults are ingrained in society. As a result I saw it as my mission to set a precedent in Rugby League. I wanted every player and official to realise if they're going to talk such trash then they'd better be prepared to be hammered and embarrassed at the highest level. Indeed, I have no doubt Robbie Simpson almost ruined his career at St George by standing beside me during the racial hailstorm. It wasn't until I resigned from the Dragons that he was promoted back to the top grade and that came after months of watching St George-Illawarra struggle to find their form. It angered me to see Robbie languish in first division despite being acknowledged as one of the club's best defenders.

The Human Rights Commission sent an officer to oversee the hearing at the NRL's base at Fox Studios and he heard how Ward had supposedly directed the remark at Robbie in retaliation for being called a 'fat c***'. I vehemently disputed that and am still adamant his comment was intended to rattle me. For two-and-a-half hours the sub-committee—comprising John

Brass, Kevin Brasch and Malcolm Noad—heard both sides of the story and they formed the view that *if* the comment was made and I heard it, then I was entitled to be offended. Ward was found guilty of breaching the game's NRL racial vilification policy and they imposed a $10,000 fine—which was believed to be the highest fine ever placed on a professional Australian sportsman for such an offence. Ward offered the media throng a strong 'no comment', but the Bulldogs' boss Bob Hagan voiced his opinion, saying, 'I'm absolutely disgusted but I've been told not to comment.' I was asked during the examination by the Bulldogs' solicitor whether I thought Canterbury was a racist club, but I didn't bite. However, Hagan's reaction annoyed me. He said he was disgusted. At what? The code's decision to take a stance against a racist remark?

The reaction was varied. John MacDonald from the *Australian* called me a 'silly sausage' and went on to say my words have spoken louder than my actions and that I was beating myself with silly stunts. David McNicoll, a respected columnist from *The Bulletin*, told his readers: 'the fine must rank as one of the most asinine decisions in the history of sport. If Mundine had called another player a "white c***", would the sporting authorities have fined him $10,000?'

However, on matters of race and humanity McNicholl's magazine has a poor track record. In its formative years in the 1800s it reflected the redneck nature of the colonial days. Indeed on 9 June 1883 *The Bulletin* proposed this as a way to help 'solve' the Aboriginal problem:

Gather them all together in an immense reserve in North-Western Australia; say there is plenty of room there. Let them have no rum and no religion, but fight and frolic in their own way, they would have reduced their own numbers so much by internal quarrels that the boundary line of their reservations could be shifted inwards far enough to allow four or five 'runs' in the space vacated. So the process of closing in could go on until the last survivors, two or three in number, were frozen out altogether. Some showman by that time would make a good thing of taking them around the other colonies and exhibiting them as curiosities. This is the way to let the black race die out easily and naturally.

The NRL gave the Bulldog forward the right to appeal against the severity of the sentence and on hearing it they reduced the fine by 50 per cent. And then the final insult came when the NRL said Ward would have to pay if he violated the racial vilification law the following year. The Bulldogs offered to pay the $5000 on Ward's behalf, and under the *Daily Telegraph*'s headline 'Fined $10,000 for racial slur but . . . Ward won't pay a cent' the journalist trumpeted that the NRL board reduced the fine to $5000 and stipulated the remaining $5000 would be paid only if Ward reoffended next season. This decision was made given the 'circumstances', including Ward's attempts to conciliate, his contrition and his financial circumstances.

Obviously I was disappointed by the NRL's about-face in letting Ward walk virtually scot-free. I read their statement over and over, and all I could ask was who the hell was the victim? And what kind of message did it send out to the wider community? I'd fought for the right cause; I tried to stop an ugly disease that's tearing the country apart and even now I can't help but feel the NRL kicked me up the backside. I didn't hide my disappointment. It was an anger which wouldn't subside and after I sprayed the Bulldogs with the 'racist' tag in the lead up to our clash in 1999, Hagan told the *Telegraph* the NRL should look at fining me for bringing the game into disrepute!

The Bulldogs ultimately decided against pursuing their threatened legal action but Hagan did issue a strongly worded statement to the press:

> Canterbury does not need to request the NRL to take action against Anthony Mundine for breach of the NRL rules relating to making public comments detrimental to the interests and welfare of the game. The NRL has always taken action of this type and does not propose to intervene in the normal process. Canterbury would nevertheless like to place on record its views that the continual comments made by Mundine are far more damaging to the image of the game than the action currently being contemplated by the NRL concerning critical comments about the performances of referees.

# FLIGHT AND FIGHT

# CHAPTER 19

# GONE WALKABOUT

*My advice to the boy is to drop out of Rugby League. He should give it away and relax.*
My father to Channel 10, 25 April 2000.

*He's been under a lot of pressure and if there is anything we can do, we're here and available. I hope he can then come back to the NRL because the NRL will be poorer without him.*
NRL Chief Executive, David Moffett, 27 April 2000

When I missed selection in the Australian team for the 2000 Anzac Test, it dawned on me that I'd gone as far as an outspoken Aborigine could go in a repressive sport. That revelation was like an electric charge and I asked myself whether it was worth my while to pursue a dream I was never going to achieve—to wear the green and gold. In all honesty that moment of enlightenment left me feeling empty, because in three consecutive weeks I'd come up against the premiership's top five-eighths—Brad Fittler, Laurie Daley and Matthew Johns—and I'd whipped them. However, even those performances weren't enough to get me into the national team. It wasn't as if I didn't have any supporters in the weeks leading up to the Trans-Tasman international. Test coach Chris Anderson made it crystal clear that I'd be a more than valuable asset for the squad, and I also received word from Arthur Beetson (via a friend) that his advice for me to make the Australian team was to lift my defence—so I did. I tackled my heart out.

However, twenty-four hours before the selectors gathered, I could feel it in my bones that I was going to be again overlooked. Instead of waiting to be kicked in the guts I made a phone call, and on the Sunday the selectors were due to name their team, they woke to read on the back page of the *Sun Herald*: **'I WHIP HIM . . . SO WHY PICK HIM—Mundine attacks "golden boy" Fittler.'** I told reporter Danny Weidler that the selectors' blind favoritism would ensure Fittler was picked in the Australian team. Then I said:

> At the end of the day they all know who 'the man' is . . . the selectors, my rivals and the public. Fittler will be selected in the side because it is very hard to beat the golden boy. In reality I should be in the side. He would know that what we have going isn't a rivalry. I don't see it as a rivalry. He hasn't beaten me or outplayed me in the last five years. I have whipped him every time. Is he the benchmark for selection or not? By the selectors he has been considered the one for the job. If I beat him year after year, why isn't that rewarded? My so-called rivals have not come close to me. From 1996 to this year I have not been beaten. That is a complete domination. Is that a rivalry? I call it a mismatch . . . I have nothing personal against Fittler or anyone for that matter, I just don't like injustice being done.

My fury was, in part, fuelled by Fittler's volunteering to pack down at lock so Matthew Johns could fill in at five-eighth, and that came on top of Laurie Daley's call for the Newcastle pivot to get the nod ahead of me! Sure enough, when the selectors met I didn't get the nod. I was overlooked—although, it has been suggested to me that Anderson's dream team from lock to five-eighth read Brad Fittler (13), Brett Kimmorley (7) and Anthony Mundine (6). But the selectors, headed by Eddie Lumsden and John Raper, are said to have told Anderson that if he wanted Kimmorley, Fittler had to wear the number 6 jumper, which meant I was left right out.

Look, I didn't expect to be in the team, but when I was snubbed those old demons started dancing about in my head—politics with a capital 'P'. On my mother's fridge is a cartoon which appeared in the Koori press when Nathan 'Tinga' Blacklock, David Peachey and I were overlooked for the 1999 Australian Tri-series team. The cartoonist has illustrated Nathan and I consoling one another with Tinga asking, 'What sort of credentials do you need to represent the Australian side? Play in a grand final? Score 24 tries, winger of the year, a promoter's dream, or antics on the field to please the public. No it's none of them. So it's a joke!' In the cartoon I'm seen replying, 'Yes, it seems you need to be suspended for taking performance-enhancing drugs or expose yourself to a female, assault someone, or, in our case, it depends on the colour of your skin.'

I looked at that cartoon a few times in the aftermath of the Anzac Test team's announcement and figured I'd had enough of it all. It was time to step into the boxing ring and prove myself in the most gladiatorial sport of all—a sport where a man's two fists are his best friend, and your enemies are in front of you. However, I needed time alone to collect my thoughts and, in the true spirit of a 'walkabout', I looked to see where I could get away from everyone to 'chill'. It seemed the right thing to do. After all, my shoulder was still injured, so I wasn't able to play.

I thought of going to the deep heart of the Northern Territory and the solitude of northern New South Wales but that wasn't far away enough for me. I instead looked towards the US, where I could stay with friends who knew—and cared—

very little about Rugby League. The *Sun Herald* blew the whistle on my escape plans. In the wake of the Dragon's 28–20 win over Penrith the *Herald* reported I had not only failed to turn up to watch the game at the Sydney Football Stadium but that my bags were packed and I was ready for an overseas flight. 'If Mundine takes the flight he will go overseas to chill out,' the *Sun Herald* noted. 'It is thought he needs time away from everyone to sort out a few issues which have been bugging him. Mundine has told his parents that he needs a break. It is known that Mundine is disillusioned with elements in the game, including racism.'

While the Rugby League fraternity tried to work out where I was and what I was planning, I was holed up in my Cronulla apartment, bags packed, return airticket in hand. On Tuesday morning, the day a battalion of journalists descended upon Steelers Stadium to see if I fronted, my gang transported me to Sydney Airport, and one of them, Codey, checked my luggage in at the Qantas counter. The person manning the desk took a look at the name on the ticket and demanded to see me; I can only hazard a guess it was a security thing. He came to the car and found me talking on my mobile. He was extremely helpful and, after doing everything to ensure I was checked in quickly to avoid detection, he shook hands and said, 'I'm sure I'll be reading about this.'

Before boarding the flight I tried to phone my mate and Saints skipper, Nathan Brown, to inform him of my plans and I left a message on his mobile. I was to later learn, however, that Browny lost his mobile on the Gold Coast—which meant he was in the dark when the media started phoning. With that, I was off into the wild blue yonder to find an answer to the biggest question of my sporting career: should I quit Rugby League?

When the media turned up to the Dragons' training session and discovered I wasn't there, the Sydney rumour mill went into overdrive with 'sightings' in Hawaii, western New South Wales, Miami, Quebec, Darwin, Mecca, Jerusalem and England. I don't know how true this rumour is, but I'm told when the press became even more desperate to get the scoop News Limited put a $35,000 bounty on my head for the photographer who managed to obtain an exclusive snap of me chilling. They had no hope, because while they were searching the major cities I was with a great family, the Venturas, in San Jose, a few hours south of San Francisco, who I first met when I was billeted out to them during a basketball tour in 1990. We kept in touch; they're special people—beautiful folk, really—and had no problems with me staying at their home to get things sorted out in my mind. The media meanwhile made up their story as they went along and, in what I can only think was an attempt to discredit me, one newspaper made out I was in Hawaii sunning myself on a beach while my Dragon team-mates were training in the south coast slush. The truth is I didn't even step on the sand in Honolulu. I only stopped off there briefly en route to Vancouver before flying south to San Francisco. I just chilled out in the US, shopped, saw movies and spent numerous hours thinking about my future.

It wasn't so peaceful on the home front. Mum and Dad were hounded at all hours of the day by people wanting to know the latest from the 'frontline'. In darker moments, some people feared I was close to the edge—suicidal—because the pressure had become too much for me. It was crazy, but Dragons' managing director Bob Millward helped stir that pot by telling the press he feared the club might have someone in a state and needing help. That was rubbish. At no time was I crumbling inside; at no time did I ever feel mentally weak. Believe me, to have done something as drastic as harming myself would have gone against all the things I've stood for. The answer to the Aboriginal plight isn't suicide. Instead we have to stand and fight. We have to raise ourselves above the turmoil and the trauma— there's no easy way out.

My critics called me the Invisible Man, the Running Man and Man Overboard, but what my detractors didn't realise was that their jibes only made me stronger, made me want to make them eat their words. The *Daily Telegraph*'s Paul Kent went as far as to suggest my flight to the US was a 'cry for help', saying, 'For some time now he's carried a persecution complex, claiming he hasn't been picked in representative teams because he is either (a) too outspoken, or, (b) an Aborigine.' Former Dragons' international Ian Walsh said it was time the club gave up on me, saying he was sick of my antics. 'He is a guy who plays only for himself and I would think that puts himself on the outer with his team-mates.' The *Daily Telegraph*'s Dean Ritchie was sent to talk to some of my relatives at the Aboriginal settlement of Baryulgil, near Grafton, and my uncle Leon echoed the words of so many people when he said, 'I don't think he should say too much because the media take things out of proportion. He should shut his mouth and do his talking on the field.'

A few team-mates, especially Lance Thompson and Craig Smith, came out and bagged me. But rather than dwell on their failings, I prefer to talk about the likes of Browny and my old coach David Waite. Nathan told the press he was certain I'd played my last game of Rugby League and he described it as a tragedy. In anticipation of my retirement he wrote in *Rugby League Week*:

Anthony was an excitement machine who brought people through the gates. Down here we are coached to a structure, then encouraged to 'play what you see'. Nobody in the game was better at ad-lib football than 'Choc', and even the people who bagged him for what he said would probably agree with that . . . I honestly don't know if Anthony Mundine will be back, but I do know that we will not be as dangerous without him.

It seems to me David Waite was about the only person who understood where I was coming from. When people were calling for me to be fined or dismissed from the club, David made the point that fines weren't an issue for me. He realised I had personal issues to resolve and I understand it was David who urged the club to give me time to think things out before reacting. He's a good man. David not only has a good heart but he can read people very well. And he was dead right. My escape was never about money; greed doesn't appeal to me. And I was quite prepared to face whatever fine—even the $100,000 mentioned in the *Daily Telegraph*—the board imposed on me.

Nevertheless, I had serious issues to sort out. A poll in the *Daily Telegraph* helped me realise I had my back to the wall. The punters returned a 2–1 verdict for me to be axed. And on another front I learned I didn't make the New South Wales Origin side. While chief selector Eddie Lumsden, an old winger from a long gone era, said my name had been mentioned in dispatches, he maintained, 'We didn't know where he was. That made it hard to pick him.' I'm assured he laughed at his own joke.

Still, I knew I was in for a tough couple of days when I returned from the US, but by the time I climbed aboard QF4 to return to Sydney I had pretty much decided if anyone was going to dictate the terms of The Man's future, it would be me. Not Bob Millward. Not the board. Not public polls. Me.

# CHAPTER 20

# THE MAN HAS LANDED

*Ali probably wouldn't have survived Australian knockers. Let's hope Anthony Mundine can.*

Miranda Devine, the Daily Telegraph, 3 May 2000

I expected a huge press contingent to greet me when I disembarked from the jet. As I waited in the queue at customs, I received a call on my mobile from a friend who was among the rabble, warning me a media horde worthy of a royal tour was waiting for me. My father, uncles, cousins, friends and Dragons' coach David Waite were waiting for me in the restricted area because David knew someone high up at the airport. Each wanted me to sneak out the back door, but I refused.

In an act of defiance I made it clear I would not only walk out the front gate, but that I would hold my head high! I wanted them to see I was 'The Man' and when they saw my face the media went into a frenzy! It was like watching a pack of sharks, because they ran past the barrier which separates the public from the passengers and bombarded me with questions. My family and friends formed a human barricade around me. It was like being caught in a scrum. They were pushing and shoving. I heard questions being yelled, but it was hard to distinguish what was being asked because their words not only melted into one another, but there were plenty of distractions like television and radio microphones in my face, flashbulbs from cameras, television cameras and that constant pushing 'n' shoving.

When it started to get out of hand—there were people trip-ping over, tempers were beginning to flare and clothes were being ripped—I asked my entourage to stop so the press could get a shot, and for a brief moment, there was a feeling of calm. A reporter asked what I thought about the horde and I told the truth—I loved it! Nevertheless, all good times come to an end and I left the media behind me in a cloud of exhaust fumes from my friend's sports car. As we pulled out I was asked if I had any last words and, after saying 'See you later' and offering the peace sign, I flashed the cover of the book I carried through the mad mob: *The Greatest, MY OWN STORY*, by Muhammad Ali. Then we were off to my Mum's home for a barbecue and family get-together.

It seemed as if everyone had turned out—relatives from the bush, friends from school and my beautiful baby Jada. I con-ducted two television interviews in Mum's kitchen and vented my spleen on a number of issues, especially the call by those old Dragons to axe me from the Saints line-up. I said:

> People are calling for my sacking. Guys from the 1950s era, speaking out and saying all this negativity about me. I never run from anything. I face it head on. I'm a man. Whatever time I took out they can take out of my pay. It's not about the money. Society is built on money, built on greed. I'm not built on that kind of stuff. I'm built on humanity and bringing peo-ple together.

Such insights didn't appease some folk who tore shreds off me. However, I found some allies in people I'd never met, such as the *Daily Telegraph*'s Miranda Devine, who noted that as a tee-total non-smoker like my father, a practising Muslim and a passionate political thinker, I was a misfit in the ocker, blokey, piss-up-and-chunder, drop-your-pants-at-the-casino culture of Rugby League. She asked: 'So who should change? Not Mundine. He is a genuine role model, especially for Aborigines, not a bogus sponsor-manufactured image like so many famous sports people.'

Yeah, Rugby League had something special, but they didn't know how to hang on to it. That was in my mind when I weighed up both my future and what I wanted to tell the Dragons' Board of Directors.

# TO WHOM THIS MAY CONCERN

*For a person tossing in a $600,000-a-year job, The Man was amazingly relaxed*
*yesterday. Anthony Mundine sucked on a lollipop, smiled and cracked jokes*
*as his very eventful rugby league career comes to a premature end. He was*
*obviously comfortable with his decision.*

The Daily Telegraph's Jon Geddes, 4 May 2000

I think what upset most people about my resignation from
the Dragons was the fact I did it without shedding any tears.
If I had broken down, bawled like a baby, then maybe
some people might have found a reason to forgive me. Tears
could have been my redemption, but I wasn't looking for anyone's pity. The truth is I felt no emotion; I'd had enough of
football and decided to resign from it. In reality it was no different to someone else leaving their job because they'd lost
interest or their belief in it. Priests leave the church, politicians
leave office midway through their term, doctors sell their practice and even schoolteachers have been known to give up their
vocation. Yet, because I was leaving a football team—*and*
*that's all it was*—I was howled down for such things as disloy-
alty, betrayal, a lack of grace and absence of class along with
other stinging accusations.

Look, I was honest, and if that is a crime then toss me in a
prison cell. Had I so desired, I could have stuck it out at
St George-Illawarra until the end of the season, copped their
cash for three months and just cruised, baby. And it wasn't as if

I was turning my back on peanuts either, because I was sacrificing big cash. However, so strong was my desire to be true to myself, and to the club, I rejected a couple of hundred thousand dollars—a point that was overlooked when people started casting their caustic comments at me. Their views meant little to me, however, because I know if *they* were offered a better position or they'd had enough of their current job, then they wouldn't be seen for their dust! It's a real pity that people are so quick to judge. Those same people phoned the club—and some of them weren't even Dragons fans—to urge the hierarchy to sack me *and* fine me $100,000. Their cold-hearted condemnation of me was actually an indictment of them, and I pray for them.

David Waite knew of my decision an hour before I made it official. I'd spoken to him and former chief executive Brian Johnston the day before to sound them out and see how I would be received at Kogarah. When I realised I was truly lost to the game, however, I phoned and apologised to David for any inconvenience I'd put him to because David Waite is one of the greatest people I've met—not only in football, but everyday life. I pay homage to Waite as a man and a coach. While many coaches are called 'gurus' and 'masterminds' David is a cut above them all in my book—*this book*—because I've seen him take a team to two grand finals when, by rights, they shouldn't have even been in the hunt. David has the rare knack of knowing how to make a team 'click' and I think it says plenty for him that when Noel Goldthorpe, Scott Gourley, Jason Stevens, Nick Zisti, Kevin Campion, Troy Stone, David Barnhill and I left Kogarah Oval at the height of the Super League war, the club didn't become a paper tiger. Instead St George remained a real contender; that was thanks to the strategies of my mate and coach David Waite, who had also guided us to the 1996 Grand Final after being handed the reins when coach-designate Rod Reddy left to take charge of the now defunct Super League franchise the Adelaide Rams.

I relocated to Brisbane after Manly beat us in the 1996 Grand Final and I trekked north with a heavy heart, brother. I'd never experienced a disappointment like it on the sporting field before, and it felt as if my heart had been ripped out of my chest and drop-kicked into the neighbouring Sydney Cricket Ground. Gritty Sea Eagles halfback Geoff Toovey engineered the win, but the media honed in on referee David Manson allowing Sea Eagles' fullback Matthew Ridge to regain his feet after he appeared tackled. It became an issue because Manly scored an all-important try from the very next ruck! While it wasn't to be the last grand final controversy I experienced—the 1999 one, when Melbourne was awarded a penalty try in controversial circumstances was a shocker—I was devastated. The pain of defeat hurt big time and one of my most poignant memories from that last Sunday in September of 1996 was David taking time out of his own disappointment to give me a hug because I looked *that* shattered.

While I know my name won't be appearing on too many St George invitation lists (and that doesn't concern me in the slightest), I do have some fond memories and great friendships from those days. Brian Johnson is one of the friends. Had he not been forced to step down from his post as chief executive because of health reasons, there is every chance I would have seen the season out. Brian was as much a friend as a loyal leader. When I stood up to be counted against the racist remark made by that Bulldogs player in 1999, he stood by me and I won't ever forget it. And while he is on the road to recovery, I hope Brian realises he is in my prayers and that when I think of him I smile. The junior development officer Max Innis is also a special dude. He discovered me as a scrawny, quiet kid and watched over me as I established myself in the big league. And then there have been the team-mates I have shed blood with, like my old skipper Mark Coyne. He was a great footballer, and like many supporters I was touched when he decided to donate the $250,000 he made during his testimonial season with the Dragons to help sick kids. It was an almighty gesture and it says a lot for the quality and decency of the man. Mark has had a big impact on my life, and I thank him for that. I have other friends in the club too including my two cousins Wes Patten and Amos Roberts. Then there's Nathan Brown, Nathan Blacklock and Wayne Bartrim, to name a few. My brotherly love is with them, I wish them peace now and forever.

While I have turned my back on the club, I'm not totally anti-St George. My bond with the club stretches back to my days in the Harold Matthews Shield. The club saw something in me, and they gave me a thousand dollar scholarship and in time the club helped to teach me what my worth as a person—and foot-baller—was. I can't thank them enough for that, because knowing who you are transcends any bank balance or invest-ment portfolio. It is through my association with the Dragons that I developed a profile which allows me to go to schools and even prisons to rap with people who need a bit of a lift and some inspiration. Believe it or not, playing for St George also played an important part in my realising and embracing my Aboriginality. When I first made my way to Kogarah Oval as a lower grader all the 'brothers'—Jeff Hardy, Ricky Walford, Andrew Walker, me, and a few of the other coloured players, would 'chill' in a part of the dressing room which became known as 'Koori Corner'. We'd talk about life and other issues and in my mind's eye I still see that as a special time in my life.

My one criticism of St George, apart from what I see as Illawarra trying to take over the running of the place, and that's

CHAPTER 21 - To Whom This May Concern

something the board will need to watch, is the fact that most of its people live in the past. It stares down at you from the great portraits and you hear it in the elderly supporters' voices. The deeds of the teams from the 1950s and 1960s still dictate the club's direction—and that can be disheartening for the team trying to follow in their footsteps. People have asked me since I left the club how I would feel if I bumped into Johnny Raper, probably my harshest critic, in the street now I'm 'independent'. Well, I'd hope he could look me in the eye, because that's exactly how I'd treat him. I have no reason to cringe and, despite our run-ins, nor does he. Nevertheless, in the wake of my departure there were cries from Craig Smith for me to be 'a man, and apologise' but I have no reason to explain myself to him, or to anyone for that matter. Smith made a name for himself out of my departure from the Dragons, he's seen as a straightshooter—and it's my great hope he can take the step up and prove himself on the field. There are rumours he whacked me early in the 2000 season, and all I can say is that story was the figment of someone's imagination, and its purpose was to put me down and make me look bad.

After bagging me in the press Lance Thompson phoned to say his comments against me during my departure weren't personal—but I can't help but feel as if my old schoolmate knew he was putting the boot into me whenever he opened his mouth. The fact Lance spoke up a storm when he should have remained quiet is the reason I admire my mates like Nathan Blacklock and Nathan Brown; they waited to see what the story was rather than joining the lynching party. And when sections of the club turned on me, Browny stood tall when he refused to join the mob. When they asked for his feelings about me he told the press, 'I'm not going to come out and bag Anthony—I don't bag my mates. My mum and dad didn't bring me up like that. Anthony's my mate and Anthony chose to do what he wanted.' In my way of thinking it's that type of sentiment which makes Nathan Brown a saint among the Saints.

Look, I don't know how the board really felt when they learned I was giving the game away. I'm certain some were relieved, but I'd like to think other members, like my friend Doug McClelland, felt sorry to see me leave. I'm certain some of them, the Illawarra crowd, figured I was going to beg for another chance, plead to be seen as being worthy. But there was no chance of that. I'd set my mind's course and after being informed of my intentions by coach Waite they were waiting with a deed of termination. The formalities took a mere ten minutes.

I turned up to our appointment late because my car had run low on petrol. After filling the tank up with juice, I went to pay and out of nothing but sheer instinct I bought a cherry Chuppa Chup. I was slurping on it when I parked the car in the Leagues club and it was still in my mouth when McClelland addressed the press. It might sound dumb, but I didn't even think twice about it. The lollipop wasn't a statement; it wasn't a show of contempt. It was nothing more than a sweet. Though my detractors, like journalist Mike Gibson, seized on it:

Tell me anyone . . . who struts around with a lollipop sticking out of the side of his mouth? And the interjection to Doug McClelland, chairman of St George-Illawarra, as he demonstrated the generosity of spirit and style of that great club, by wishing Anthony well on his retirement from Rugby League. 'He has proved himself to be a gifted footballer and athlete,' the former federal senator said. '. . . and The Man,' chimed in Anthony with a silly smirk. The lollipop. The smart-arse interjection. Think about it, Anthony. These are the images you left us with last week. Whatever you're trying to tell us, it ain't working.

Clearly, Gibson would have liked to have seen tears. The lollipop sent out the wrong message, but I felt cool and in control. When I sat down, with my father flanking me, I looked at the serious faces of the media contingent and decided to break the ice. 'Obviously you're all here about the saga that went on when I took time out to come to terms with my future and what I think is best for me.' And then with a deadpan expression I continued, 'Well, all I can say is the board fined me $100,000 . . . ' Poor old Bob Millward, when he saw it wasn't going to script, he turned as pale as a ghost! He had no idea what was happening, and he didn't look happy. Then, after a pregnant pause I continued, 'From today onwards I'll no longer be a part of Rugby League. I've retired and I will be holding a press conference, probably Friday, to reveal all the unanswered questions. To the people I didn't get to who are close to me, I'm sorry and I'll be talking to every one of you when I get the opportunity.'

Doug started his spiel, but his words seemed to run into each other because I wasn't listening to a lot of it, I was looking at the press and watching them scribble down every word. I wondered what they were thinking—they probably thought I was mad to turn my back on the cash. Some, I thought, would be sad to be losing a regular headline. My trance was broken when I heard Doug mention some of my virtues as a footballer, and towards the end of his tribute I piped up 'and The Man' (the interjection Gibson complained about) because that's how I want to be remembered by Doug and the board. With that, I walked out of the club without even looking back. And boy, it felt as if I'd had the weight removed from my shoulders. It felt as if I could fly! As I drove off to my new life, David Waite tried to explain my character to the media horde: 'We don't have a history of professional sport in our country, unlike America, and Europe and England. Professional sports need stars and they need good players as well, and obviously Anthony thought he was in those two brackets and he told people that.' The *Sydney Morning Herald*'s Brad Walter simply commented: 'One thing is for certain, Rugby League is likely to become more mundane without Mundine.'

One of the sad postscripts to my departure from the Dragons was the demise of David Waite as coach. His sacking didn't surprise me at all. I think David may have paid a hefty price for supporting me when the Dragons' board wanted my blood during my American odyssey. His show of sympathy was appreciated by me and made even more special when he told the press that if his standing by me in my time of need was part of the reason for his being overlooked for a new contract, then he had no regrets. Indeed, he even suggested some people might want to look at their level of compassion. If anything, the way David was treated only served to highlight the kind of people I had opposed in my last days with the club. They crucified a decent man and they should be ashamed.

# CHAPTER 22

# BOXED IN

*Boxing is the sport to which all other sports aspire.*
*Former world heavyweight champion George Foreman*

**W**hen I announced I was going to box I spared a thought for my mother because I know she loathes the sport. However, like the rest of my family, Mum accepted my decision as my own and she's vowed to stand beside me. She did it for Dad thirty years ago, and she's promised to do it for me.

Boxing is a sport. The rest, including Rugby League, are mere games. When a man climbs the three steps which lead into the square ring he's butt-naked. There's no escaping the glare of the crowd, there is no avoiding your opponent and when the heat's on, baby, and the punches are snapping the life out of you there's nowhere to run. In Rugby League players get to hide on the interchange bench or wide of the rucks when they're struggling. But in boxing if you drop your hands—POW—you're out like a light. The opponents are more often than not perfect physical specimens of the human species and it's what I call a colour-blind sport because the best man always wins. Sure, it sometimes might not be reflected on the scoresheet, but in their heart-of-hearts the fighters know who really won and who really lost.

For all its glory, however, boxing is also a sport of contradictions. On one hand, boxing can take a nobody and catapult him to superstardom; yet, on the other hand it can pulverise a man and punch every ounce of hope and intelligence from him. But I think the tempting of fate is what makes the sport so attractive to me—like parachuting, it's a challenge in which you have to overcome your doubts and fears. My father openly admits there's a dark side to boxing—and, man, when he talks about it, it sounds like one hell of a bitch.

'Boxing is a sad sport, brother,' he told the *Sunday Telegraph* in 1989. 'In the ring there is no place to hide and there can only be one winner. It's a sad sport.'

I know where my father's thoughts stem from because while he's savoured the sweet taste of victory he's also spat the bitter pill of defeat from his mouth. However, I see boxing as a noble sport. It's gladiatorial and gracious and it is my plan to bring the world super-middleweight title to the family home. The idea of winning the world title really excites me. And, while I admire Fenech as a fighter, I can't understand why he once said he'd give up his world titles for an Australian Rugby League jumper. The League jumper is certainly a great trophy but the world title, man, it's universal. To be the world champion is to say you're the best of the best—you're The Man—and I wouldn't hesitate to swap my League achievements just for a chance at winning a belt.

I also think boxing will allow me be to be a better representative for my people. Rugby League has allowed me to get a foothold but it's not an international sport. No-one in America or Chile or China knows about Rugby League, but they all love boxing and they respect the warriors. While Muhammad Ali is mobbed by crowds wherever he goes, I reckon outside of New South Wales, Queensland and a pocket of Northern England, few people would know of Rugby League immortal Johnny Raper.

At the beginning of the 2000 NRL season Sydney's Channel Ten reported I was considering severing my ties with Rugby League at the end of the season—I did it halfway through—to pursue a professional boxing career and it created plenty of interest. Everywhere I went, be it a coffee shop or even footy training I was asked whether I was *really* going to turn my back on $600,000 to start an apprenticeship in the most brutal of sports. Well, I have. I believe I have it in me to go all the way as a boxer because I have the moves, the punches, the background and the genetics. Apart from Dad, his brothers and Mum's brothers also fought and I've inherited their passion, their hunger and their heart. Indeed some people, including Dad's former cornerman and assistant trainer Ern McQuillan Jnr (Ern Snr was his trainer), believe I'd make a better fighter than footballer—and Ernie knows his business. In 1990, the late Ray Connelly, who saw some of the world's greatest fight in the capacity of a ring announcer, wrote about me in the *Sydney Morning Herald*: 'He regards both basketball and League as simply fun and pastimes to be enjoyed, but it is different when it comes to boxing, the only sport he wishes to take seriously.' And when it became public knowledge a few years ago that I considered scrapping footy to try and make the Olympic boxing team, Fenech's old trainer, Johnny Lewis, said he thought I'd make a good fist of it—however, I canned the plan when Cathy Freeman's old sparring partner, Arthur Tunstall, who is president of the Australian Amateur Boxing Association, suggested I was kidding myself. With him offside I knew I had no hope of boxing at the Games so I abandoned the idea. By the way, can anyone give me Arthur's boxing record?

Some people, such as Aussie Joe Bugner, thought I was certifiable for abandoning the big money and security of Rugby League for the great unknown, but that isn't a worry. Dad has

the contacts in Australia and abroad, while my profile as a
Rugby League player created plenty of interest when I stepped
into the ring. I want to take the world on in boxing gloves and
nothing quite gave my plans such a mighty boost as the time I
met a homeless black American in the early hours in New York
City a couple of years ago. My good mate 'Abs'—a mate from
Lebanon—and I were out painting NYC red, white and blue.
We'd been to a nightclub in Brooklyn but moved on because it
had way too much attitude. After passing airport-type security
just to get into the place we found it to be like something out
of a movie set; it wasn't the place to be if you didn't have the
right moves. We hit the road and at 4 a.m. we roamed around
42nd Street, 44th Street and Madison Square Garden—one of the
globe's great boxing venues. I shadow-sparred on the steps of
the place and as I speared my lefts and rights with a champion's
precision I screamed, 'I'll be back baby! I'll be back and I'm
gonna be the champion of the world!'

It felt so real, and as we made our way back to our hotel a
homeless black man confronted us. He looked as if he had seen
a lot of life and he asked what kind of athlete I was. He said I
had an athlete's physique and I took it as a compliment. I told
him I played Rugby League in Australia, and while he hadn't
heard of the game something flickered in his eyes—he'd worked
out I was an Aborigine and yelled, 'You're a brother from Australia!' It's funny how the repressed have an instant bond and he
smiled when I said I'd return to Madison Square Garden and
fight for the world title. The old man, who'd been touched by
Ali, nodded wisely when I told him the world champion's belt
would help give my people even greater pride. Before going our
separate ways he said if I were to train for a boxing career I had
to follow the old fashioned methods—the honest ways like running up and down stairs and doing thousands of sit-ups. 'Just

don't give up, never give up,' he said, before disappearing into the shadows.

When I was a teenager I had four amateur fights in the French outpost of Noumea for as many wins. Two by knockout and two on points, and my style clearly made an impression on a few French boxing identities, because they wanted me to relocate to Paris and stage my quest for a world title from there. Instead I embraced Rugby League, but what I have found is while I had no nerves in Rugby League, there's a real fear which accompanies you into the boxing ring—the fear of defeat, of pain, of being humiliated and of letting yourself down. The challenge is to rise above this and keep your composure once the bell sounds because if you don't, well, you're just another piece of meat about to be put through the sausage mincer.

Boxing really is in my heart and, apart from those four amateur fights, I have fought a couple of exhibition bouts in Brisbane and Sydney. My first bout in the pro ring occurred at one of Dad's favourite slaughterhouses, Brisbane's Festival Hall, when I aimed up against South Africa's Justice 'The Judge' Ganiza. I was in Brisbane to play for the Broncos' Super League championship winning team and the club didn't mind me toying with the sport, I figure because the engineers behind Super League thought it was good publicity for their cause. It was only a bit of fun and I didn't mind playing the clown. At one stage I even kissed Ganiza on the cheek while in a clinch! The *Sun Herald*'s ringside correspondent wrote: 'On the odd occasion he stopped waltzing and started sparring there were signs he had inherited the skills that took his dad to eight titles.' Nice wrap. My other bout was fought in 1995 at Marrickville Town Hall against Troy Speed just after I cancelled my professional debut to focus on playing football for the Dragons. However, I remember waking up that very next morning wanting to put the gloves on, but as I told the *Sunday Telegraph* there were problems try-ing to combine the two: 'It's different training and you need a different body. To play footy you try to bulk up, but with box-ing you have to trim down to make the weight.'

Rugby League is a volatile sport, but the rules have been designed to curb players from going for each other with their fists and I think that's a shame because while I'm not for wan-ton violence, I know I'd want to see a bit of biffo if I was a punter in the stands. I've reacted to a few on-field incidents by shaping up to opponents who have tried to intimidate me, but few have been willing to tango. You can tell when a game of footy is about to erupt—you can smell it—and your frustrations come to the surface. What the people who control the game must realise is people don't want to see a catty little game, they want full-on action—and that can involve the odd free-for-all.

At the beginning of the 1998 season the *Sunday Telegraph* rated Rugby League's top ten fighters and I headed the list, with my good mate Solomon a close second. Solo, who really is a gentle giant, confirmed he had what it takes when he bombed Dan Stains, a black belt in martial arts, during a blood 'n' thun-der Balmain–Manly match in 1996. The Brookvale crowd, normally bayers for blood, turned their heads in horror. Stains is the first to admit he went looking for the fight and, credit to his character as a man, Dan later apologised to Solomon for pushing him past the point of no return; it's clear on video footage my blood brother wanted no trouble. The article rated the top ten knucklemen and the list went like this:

**LEAGUE'S TOP 10 FIGHTERS**
**Anthony Mundine (St George)**
**Solomon Haumono (Canterbury)**
**Terry Hill (Manly)**

**Paul Harragon (Newcastle)**
**David Furner (Canberra)**
**Ian Roberts (North Queensland)**
**James Pickering (Sydney City)**
**Les Davidson (Cronulla)**
**Jarrod McCracken (Parramatta)**
**Craig Greenhill (Cronulla)**

Now I have made the leap from footy to fighting I'll liaise with the dudes who have done well in the sport of kings—Lionel Rose, Fenech, Kostya Tszyu, Glenn and Kevin Kelly and Troy Waters. I'll also be relying big time on Dad for his guidance. My campaign will be full on and calculated. And don't think I can't do it. If I set my mind to something then I break down walls to achieve it.

My confidence has, however, upset some people, including the world rated light-heavyweight Glenn Kelly who told the press he wanted to knock me cold because I was showing him a lack of respect by saying I intend to take the boxing world by storm! At the time of his comments Kelly was highly rated by the International Boxing Federation (IBF) and the World Boxing Association (WBA); he was undefeated in twenty-four bouts and the American-based promoter Cederic Kushner wanted him to sign a twelve-fight deal. With his credentials, I'm happy to say I admire Glenn Kelly as a fighter and I like him as a man, too. Like too many boxers in this country he's achieved a tremendous amount but he's received little recognition for his efforts. I think he knew he'd make headlines by challenging me, and that's cool, I can live with it. The media was keen for we two successful Aborigines to collide—Glenn is a brother—because one of us would walk away triumphant and the other a loser. Look, Glenn could go all the way and I would be one of the

first to congratulate him; even though we'll be in different
weight divisions I'll be more than glad to tangle with him if it
means I'll get to where I'm headed quicker. This is what Kelly
told the *Sunday Telegraph*'s Cameron Bell, and his words have
only added extra fuel to my desire burning within:

> I'm just sick of the way he is carrying on . . . Choc has never
> come out and said my name, but who else would he be talking
> about when he says he can beat anyone in Australia . . . It's got
> back to me that he's told people he can beat any light-
> heavyweight in Australia with one hand tied behind his back.
> Well, how about fighting me—I'm the champion . . . If someone
> put a fight together between me and Choc I'd knock him out.
> I've proved I'm the best and he hasn't proved anything . . . Say-
> ing he will be too good for anyone if he went to boxing is like
> me saying I'll go back to football and be a better five-eighth
> than him . . . If he wanted to jump in the ring with me, I'd knock
> him out and teach him to stay in his own sport . . . I'm just sick
> of him shooting his mouth off—he is in a dreamland . . . I've
> proven myself and he hasn't—it's that simple. I respect him as
> a footballer but from what he has said it's clear he doesn't
> respect me as a boxer . . . First it was a gold medal at the
> Olympics he wanted and now it's a world title . . . Well, I'm
> closer to the world title than he'll ever be . . . Is it a publicity
> stunt for him or is he serious? It's just that whenever Bones [his
> world-rated brother Kevin] and myself start to get a bit of pub-
> licity about our boxing, he starts talking about what he's going
> to do and that upsets me.

And that's what I like about boxing—it's war. There's the presence of the Angel of Death—it's a sport in which you need a
sixth sense because you have to read your opponent's actions

and anticipate his next move. It's more cunning than chess because a fighter tries to manipulate his opponent into throwing the punch he wants. And to be crowned champion is to be king of the warriors. It's barbaric—punch-for-punch—and it's there twenty-four hours a day, seven days a week and for the length of your career. In Rugby League if you make a mistake you concede a few metres, or, at the very worst a try. In boxing, one error and you could wake up in hospital, or worse.

# CHAPTER 23

# MARCH OF THE GLADIATOR

*I dream I'm running down the Broadway. That's the main street in Louisville, and all of a sudden there's a truck coming at me. I run at the truck and I wave my arms, and then I take off and I'm flying. I go right up over the truck, and all the people are standing around and cheering and waving at me. And I wave back and I keep on flying.*

Cassius Clay (Muhammad Ali) 1963

**M**onday, 16 May 2000. The rest of my life begins today. This sunny day marks my first official training session, the first step towards my long campaign to a world title and I'm feeling hyped. The door to the gymnasium is locked, and as I wait out on Eveleigh Street an old man asks if I'm serious about trying to win the world super-middleweight crown. I nod. 'I wouldn't be at this gymnasium, sir, if I didn't believe I had it in me.'

The man wishes me good luck and, with that, he walks back to his own life; his own survival. After a fifteen-minute wait the door is opened and I feel a rush of adrenalin as I climb the rickety old staircase. 'This is it,' I whisper, so softly no-one hears me. 'The realisation of a long held dream.'

Not everyone shares my enthusiasm. The *Daily Telegraph*'s boxing writer Terry Smith described the super-middleweight title as one of the weakest divisions. It was a typical putdown with Smith noting, 'There is hardly a worthwhile American among the top-ranked boxers. Johnny Lewis, the trainer who took Jeff Fenech, Jeff Harding and Kostya Tszyu to world titles, believes Anthony Mundine could make the middleweight limit without too much trouble. However, this division bristles with top-line American talent.'

I've already realised I am going to have to overcome a lot of resentment and jealousy as I prove myself in the boxing game— but I'm strong, their doubt can't harm me.

When my opponent Gerrard Zohs was presented to the press they bagged the former champion of New Zealand—the critics called him a 'stiff' and worse. Yet, he was a worthy first-up opponent. He had twenty bouts under his belt and he was a much better credentialled debut opponent than Prince Naseem Hamed, Oscar De La Hoya and Mike Tyson faced.

A couple of television crews are in the gym to record my first punches, and as I bandage my hands I'm filled with a feeling of complete and utter purpose. I contemplate the path I must tread—the early bouts, the national title, the regional belt, the Commonwealth crown, and, then, a crack at world sport's ultimate trophy, and I smile. I'm well aware it will be a lonely path, but my dad has vowed to watch my *every* step. He'll be my guardian angel and knowing that gives me a supreme feeling of confidence.

In our first session on the pads I drive my gloved fist into Dad's focus mitts and with each blow I feel a surge of power which makes me feel good—at the same time, I'm well aware there is room for plenty of improvement.

And I think—I think of the journey I've undertaken to get to where I am now. It's funny, but I've rarely thought about Rugby League since turning my back on the Dragons. In all honesty, my football career seems as if it happened years ago. It's like a dream. And that makes me wonder whether it was really all that important to me. Perhaps the politics jaded me because I do remember a time, and it wasn't all that long ago, when it was such an important part of my life.

As a child I was a natural at most things I tried my hand at. I played basketball, Rugby League and boxed as an amateur. I enjoyed success in all three sports and my parents encouraged me all the way. When I was five I told my father I would one day be the world boxing champion, but back then Rugby League was also very special to me. One winter, when I represented Zetland in the South Sydney competition, Dad promised to pay me a dollar for every try I scored. By the last game of that season he'd parted with $65 and while it was the easiest money I've ever made, I didn't need such an incentive because I loved my football—I really loved it! I could really express myself out on the paddock, and with a ball in my hand I'd weave my magic and it sometimes felt as if I was dancing on air.

Yet, even on the junior football field the colour of my skin was an issue for some opponents and many was the time I would tattoo their sneering faces with black 'n' blue bruises courtesy of my solid blows. I couldn't help but take delight in hearing their harsh racist taunts turn to tearful pleas for the referee to save them from a hiding, but, as was the case in the playground, I soon learnt there was no future in fighting *every* mug. In time I concentrated on making them look small by carving them up when I had the ball in my hands and by jolting them with heavy hits when it was my turn to defend. It was the right move because when I focused purely on football and not standing over the 'baby' bigots I gained tremendous recognition from talent scouts such as St George's Max Innes.

When news reached the media that the son of the great Tony Mundine was linked with St George they phoned Max and he predicted a rosy future for me, telling the *Sunday Telegraph*,

'He can do anything. He has very good speed and ball skills and just as important, he is a very good competitor.'

It was a golden season because, after going without a single victory in three years, my team won the 1992 Jersey Flegg competition and I was picked for the New South Wales under-17s side which played Queensland, even though I was only given four minutes run-on time. Things were much better in 1993 when I was picked for both the Australian Schoolboys and Australian Joeys teams which played Great Britain's junior team, and it was such a great honour I congratulated myself on deciding to turn my back on basketball and putting my boxing aspirations on hold. There were other offers. Before I signed my scholarship deal with the Dragons the Sydney Kings' assistant coach Steve McGuigan came to our house and tried to convince Mum, Dad and I there was a future for me in the American sport. While the Kings didn't offer kids financial inducements to play, he said they could help me gain entry into the Australian Institute of Sport or even into an American college, but that wasn't for me. I moved on, much to McGuigan's disappointment, as he told the press:

> I was amazed by how good he was. As far as balance, speed and strength are concerned he is second to none for his age in Sydney. I can see that the short-term financial gain is in Rugby League but I have no doubt he could have made it as a point guard with the NBL if he was willing to do his apprenticeship. He looked to me like another Steve Carfino.

Winning has long been my obsession. If someone beat me in a friendly game of table tennis I'd go and practise alone for a week and return to beat them in the rematch. If someone scored a try against me on the footy field, I'd strike back with two. That winning streak—the killer instinct—was instilled in me by Dad from the tender age of four. While other kids were colouring in books or watching *Romper Room*, Dad would take me out back and teach me the fundamentals of Rugby League and boxing. But the greatest thing he taught me, apart from the basics, was to never, *ever* give up. It was with that type of guidance that I decided early in my life that I wasn't going to be yet another *'gunna'*—and that's not an Aboriginal word. A gunna is a person who is 'gunna' do this, 'gunna' do that. And, from seeing some of the kids around me get in serious trouble with the law, I vowed not to surrender to mediocrity or peer group pressure. I instead set myself goals and whenever I said I would do something, like make the St George junior representative teams, I worked my butt off to achieve it. Nevertheless, Dad thought I was taking too much on by playing football and basketball. After all, I was studying for my Higher School Certificate and he was adamant I wasn't doing my chances of getting a good mark any favours by spending hours on the training paddock and practice court. The crunch came, however, when I went straight to basketball training with the New South Wales team after playing in a Commonwealth Bank Cup match that same afternoon. When I dragged myself through the back door Dad told me to make up my mind; it had to be one or the other.

I decided upon Rugby League because even though the NBL—and the Kings—were enjoying a boom in popularity I figured Rugby League was the sport with the future. My decision to focus on football was rewarded less than a year later, when I was called up from the junior representative ranks to make my grade debut against the Western Suburbs reserve grade side at Campbelltown. The Dragons' then first grade coach Brian Smith said the club believed I had a future, telling journalist Jon Geddes that with Andrew Walker injured and Phil Blake and

Tony Smith in the squad to go to Melbourne for a game with Wests, it was a good opportunity to give me a shot. 'He is a really good all-round sportsman and blind Freddy could see what a talented player he is.'

While I was a quiet kid then and didn't let people know what I was thinking, my thoughts on reading coach Smith's comments were like fireworks going off in my head. The Man had been launched, and I planned to shake the conservative and boring world of Rugby League like no-one else; and, while it was fun, I have greater worlds to conquer—and there's a championship team behind me.

Apart from Dad, the man who masterminded Jeff Fenech's and Jeff Harding's rise to being world champions—Johnny Lewis—is my match-maker. The king of Australian breakfast radio, Alan Jones, negotiated the minefield of promoting my first bout, in conjunction with my mate, Khoder 'Abs' Masser. News of Alan's alliance raised a few eyebrows around town because it is no secret he is a vocal supporter of One Nation's Pauline Hanson. However, we have an arrangement—Alan won't try to bash me over the head with his beliefs, and I'll return that favour. What I do like is that he has proven his commitment in wanting to see me win the world title. Within days of our shaking hands he'd drafted a business blueprint codenamed 'Black Magic' and, I have to tell you, it had the sweet smell of success.

Alan can open doors that most people could only hope to bash their heads against. One person we were trying to contact—and we called five times a day—was proving a bit difficult, but within seconds of Alan calling him he was on the phone and begging to help. And in the lead up to my first fight Alan provided terrific ideas, like having a VIP cocktail party after the bout, and the names of guests he mentioned were from Hollywood—Russell Crowe, Tom Cruise and Nicole Kidman.

# THE MAN

Listening to Alan and my other supporters talk about such things reinforced my belief that The Man can fly. But, I also know I cannot get carried away with the outside stuff. My job is to win fights and that means I have to sleep, eat, speak and dream boxing. I don't think Australia would be keen to see an outspoken Aboriginal kid be our answer to Muhammad Ali, but I'm putting everything on the line to give it a go. I have to. There's way too much at stake—no less than my helping to give the Aborigine race some hope. Believe me, that's worth bleeding for.

# CHAPTER 24

# FIRST BLOOD

The media dismissed Gerard Zohs as having no hope, but to me he was a rock which stood between my career starting with a victory or with a defeat. Though, I must say, in the build-up to my bout, the thought of defeat *never* crossed my mind. Plenty of people were deathriding me—they paid to see me broken and beaten—but I felt an amazing sense of serenity as I counted down the hours until D-Day. I was extremely focused. While I was planning Zohs' downfall, my mother was comforted by a vision of me kayoing the Kiwi in the second round.

The night at the Sydney Entertainment Centre was everything I had planned, though my soul brother Solomon threw the proceedings into temporary chaos when a collision between him and his burly opponent Ken 'the Y2K Terminator' Fuller made the ring collapse. Once the ring was repaired, Solo terminated the Terminator with a barrage of blows. When I was called upon to enter the ring my hands were still being bandaged, and it was twelve long minutes before I made my appearance amid a path of fireworks and a cloud of smoke.

The 7500-strong crowd errupted, and among them were some of Sydney's most recognisable faces, including Test cricket skipper Steve Waugh, Olympic medallists Scott Miller and Duncan Armstrong, radio heavyweights Alan Jones and John Laws (AJ was right in my corner), actress Rachel Ward, and last, but far from least, one of my childhood heroes, Lionel Rose. Most of my friends from footballing days were in the crowd, and some of my closest friends were sitting alongside my family.

As I climbed through the ropes I promised to give them a show they'd never forget. Have no doubt about it, Zohs has plenty of ticker . . . and street smarts! After we touched gloves he threw a haymaker straight at me, but I squared up when one of my blows sent him crashing to the canvas. I didn't expect Gerard to get back up, but he did—and while he landed a few good shots on me, I never felt as though I didn't have control over the fight. I did hurt my fist, but in the fourth round, after a fearsome volley, the referee called a halt to the battle. I'd won and I was proud to hold my hands up in triumph in front of 7500 fans and 16,000 pay-per-view subscribers. They'd seen the Man flex his muscles.

A lot of the media response was positive; even a few old adversaries acknowledged I'd done well, and that alone was an achievement of a kind. My first blood was a success, a huge success, thanks to the efforts of my father, and of Khodar Nasser, Alan Jones, Brian Walsh and Paul Kind of the promotions department, Richard Barrett, and the people, the many people, who offered me their heartfelt support.

Nevertheless, I went from doing backflips to flipping out, because while I was out throwing punches and taking that first step towards realising my dreams of winning the world title, thieves broke into my mum's house and stole $9000 worth of gear from me. They stole watches, my video, a stereo, and, believe it or not, my freshly washed underwear. It angered me, but I was on too great a high to become depressed. Still, I was only glad my mother or an aunt wasn't at home when the robbery occurred, because you don't know how desperate people will react to certain situations. But I will warn any would-be thief not to target my house again, unless of course they're prepared for a rude surprise.

The robbery was a lesson, but my greatest learning experience from my debut was in the ring, where I'd tasted first blood and loved it. Some critics wrote that I was far from being of world title standard, but I'm telling them the best is yet to come. While those critics wrote poison, Foxtel saw potential—they offered me major bucks so they could broadcast my next six fights.

# LAST WORD

CHAPTER 25

# BURN BABY BURN

*We have power under the act to take any child from its mother at any stage of its life, we are going to have a population of one million blacks in the Commonwealth or we are going to merge them into our white community and eventually forget that there were any Aborigines in Australia . . .*
A.O.Neville, Chief Protector of the Aborigines in Western Australia, 1937

**W**hen Senator John Herron made his sensational claim in a leaked submission to the government that the stolen generations were nothing but a myth, he sparked a bonfire which threatens to turn into a firestorm—I'm afraid it could create a force of social destruction never before seen in Australia. His comments infuriated many Aborigines, including ATSIC leader Charles Perkins. He became so consumed by anger and frustration during his interview with the British Broadcasting Commission's World Service he warned the world-wide audience of 200 million people that Sydney would be destroyed in apocalypse-like conditions because the row would 'force direct conflict between white and black Australians'. Perkins told local reporters the lead up to the Olympics was going to be a case of 'burn, baby, burn, from now on'. He said, 'We are not going to lie down like a mongrel dog so people can come along and kick us. We are going to start biting.'

His 139 explosive words on the BBC went like this:

**CP:** We didn't want to complicate the Games. We wanted the Games to go on. All the Aboriginal people, we said let's have peaceful protests here and there. Now it's turned very nasty, ugly. It is going to be violent and we're telling all the British people: 'Please don't come over. If you want to see burning cars and burning buildings, then come over. Enjoy yourself. But if you want to come to the Games, come to the Games and go straight home again.'

**BBC:** This is strong language, Mr Perkins—burning cars, burning buildings.

**CP:** Yes. What else can you do, brother? Two hundred years the white people have taken everything from us, and we stood up to it and we've said, 'Right, do things peacefully . . . according to the law of the land, everything in a proper manner, administration and all the rest of it.' What has that got us? Nowhere.

White Australia's reaction was very swift, with people from all walks of life calling for Charlie's black hide. Yet what about Herron? How on earth could he make the incredible claim that there were no stolen generations because only a suggested 10 per cent of Aborigines were affected? He argued it took 100 per cent to make a generation; yet I too can manipulate statistics and say 100 per cent of Aborigines were affected, because when a child was wrenched away from its family it hurt parents, siblings, uncles and aunts, grandparents and cousins. Every Aboriginal family, including my own, was affected in one way or another and the scars won't go away.

Indeed, Herron's opinion and beliefs lead me to believe that from the moment A.O. Neville declared his state's 'right' to steal children from their mother's arms, this nation's leaders have been in a state of denial about the rights and presence of my people. I'm afraid it's ingrained in them and it seems none of them have any intention of looking beyond the boundaries of their own limitations and addressing the problem. I have called the politicians of this great land—*my land*—'cowards'. I believe the only way they'll remove their streak of yellow is to confront the truth, and not only accept a terrible tragedy has been committed against my kind, but shout two words from the top of Parliament House in Canberra—'We're sorry'.

Yet the government continues to talk about reconciliation, and it's a joke. We Aborigines don't need to reconcile with anyone; it's a made-up word. Why should we sit at the table and shake hands and make out we had done something wrong? The Europeans were the ones who waltzed in here and destroyed my race. They were the ones who pulled the triggers in the massacres; they're the ones who stole generations from the arms of their mums; they're the ones who just trashed sacred sites. What do we Aborigines need to apologise for? Surviving?

Dr Peter Read, one of the founders of Link Up, a system which reunites stolen children with their families, said Herron was playing with statistics when he made his claim. Dr Read said that along the Sturt Highway from 1920 to 1960 the removal rate was close to ten out of ten children. Prime Minister Howard has to realise that the sins—and the heartache—of the past won't be eased by pretending nothing has happened. Indeed, I can't help but think the likes of Howard and Herron have hijacked the Aboriginal issue and manipulated it by using 'wedge' politics, which are based on the old method of divide and conquer. Perhaps it is all a ploy—diverting attention from the GST and the constant streams of jobs going overseas by picking on the Aborigine. Yet we aren't the enemy; we're your neighbours and your brothers and sisters. While the colour of our skin is different, we Australians are united by the sky we live under and the land we depend upon. All we ask for is acceptance and understanding—and we plead that the wrongs of the last 200 years be addressed. Why won't the Prime Minister apologise? And how can he expect the forgiveness of my race when he can't apologise?

In closing this book I should say that more than a few things worry me about the state of Australia. It concerns me that a poll showed an overwhelming number of Australians don't want any apology to the Aborigines; it concerns me there is only one Aborigine, Senator Aden Ridgeway, in federal politics; and it distresses me to think race relations are going backwards. These things have to change; have to turn around. I have a dream, brothers. I have a dream the Aboriginal race will no longer merely survive but will thrive and be respected. And you know what? It's not an unattainable dream. We just need acceptance. From you.